New Testament: New Testimony

to the Skills of the Writers and First Readers

David G. Palmer

The First Edition of this Booklet was published in Sri Lanka
and launched at the Jaffna Public Library in April 2005.

This Second (revised) Edition of this Booklet with accompanying CD-ROM
(the UBS4 Greek New Testament, fully parsed and rhetorically analysed)
is published in the UK in June 2006.

British Library Cataloguing-in-Publication Data

A catalogue record for this book is available from the British Library.

0-9513661-4-9/978-0-9513661-4-1

Second Edition (with Disk), prepared for printing and published in June 2006 by
Ceridwen Press,
9 Laverstock Road, Wigston, Leicestershire, LE18 2RJ, UK
email: ceridwenpress@btinternet.com

CD-ROM prepared by Michael A. Palmer, the author's twin brother

Cover design, printing and binding of booklet and copying of disk by
Flexpress Ltd.,
5 Saxby Street, Leicester, LE2 0ND, UK

CONTENTS:

To the Librarian and Staff

of the

Jaffna Public Library

destroyed by fire
in June 1981
(with the loss of 97,000 volumes and manuscripts)

re-opened, so far without ceremony
in February 2004

sadly, not the only library in world history
that has suffered an arson attack
at the hands of a governing authority

New Testament: New Testimony

to the Skills of the Writers and First Readers

This booklet and disk present the literary structures and styles of all twenty-seven 'books' of the New Testament. This is vital information for our reading of the New Testament. It is information that is to be found in the New Testament texts. And it is information about which the church and New Testament scholars have known very little, for possibly seventeen centuries.

My literary-analytical work began at Cambridge University when I was training for the ministry. In the Spring of 1982, my interest was stirred as I started work on an Undergraduate Thesis on the Central Section of Luke's Gospel. It was in this area of the Gospel of Luke that I first became aware of much that was still to be known about the literature of the New Testament. (Scholars continued to be puzzled about the limits of this section, and they looked in vain for any common thread running through it.) For me, the project simply grew from there.

For a time, my focus was on the Gospels and Acts only. Before I left Cambridge, I knew that Mark's Gospel was likely arranged in Four Series of Seven Days, that Luke and Acts likely paralleled each other and were eleven-section chiasms and that Matthew as well as John (then, that is, at that time) were likely also eleven-section chiasms. It was on a Summer Exchange with a United Methodist Minister that I ventured further. At Sicklerville, New Jersey, in 1986, my congregation, once they learned of my work, started asking me about the Revelation to John. I had never thought till then to look seriously into that book. Reading the text for signifiers of structure, as I had learned previously with the Gospels and Acts, I very quickly established to my own satisfaction that the plan was a seven-section chiasm with seven parts per section.

In 1988, on St Luke's Day, while in ministry in Cardiff, South Wales, I self-published my developing work on the six 'Books' of the New Testament: *Sliced Bread: the Four Gospels, Acts and Revelation: their Literary Structures,* Ceridwen Press, Cardiff. ('Ceridwen' was the Welsh middle name of our baby daughter who died on St Luke's Day, 1987.) As soon as I had arrived in Cardiff from Cambridge, I applied to the University there to study for a PhD part-time. I was unsuccessful with my application. I was asked, no 'told' by the then Dean of the Theological Faculty at my interview, 'Do you expect us to write your book for you?' He thought that my work was 'already too advanced'. (Until then, I had not thought about writing a book.) But my opportunity to study for a PhD came seven years later when I was 'stationed' in Paisley, in Scotland, in 1990.

At Glasgow University, I concentrated on Mark's Gospel. The rules of Ancient Rhetoric and an approach to analysing the Greek, which I didn't know then could be called 'parsing', became the foci for the development of an analytical methodology. In 1998 I was awarded my PhD and in 1999 the work was self-published as *The Markan Matrix: A Literary-Structural Analysis of the Gospel of Mark,* Ceridwen Press, Paisley. On the back cover of the book, I put: 'This book challenges nearly all that we have ever been told about Mark's Gospel: the length and character of the Prologue, the structure of the book, its leading idea, the ending of the book, and so much more besides.'

What I learned from 'Mark' I started applying to the other Books of my earlier investigations. It was only in the last week of October 2003 that I decided to have a look at Paul's writings. I had always resisted getting involved with the Letters, primarily because of my assumption that *as* they were 'Letters' they would not have structures like the 'Books'. I just thought, nevertheless, that I'd give Romans a 'go'. It was a revelation, a complete surprise! My methodology, developed for New Testament 'book' analysis, was then applied to *all* the 'letters'. An introductory look into the letters of John and Jude gave way to a study and full analysis of Hebrews (for me, the most impressive piece of writing of the New Testament, just ahead of Romans). Within a few weeks, the work (of a first full parsing and rhetorical analysis) had been completed. I and II Corinthians were the last to be done.

This booklet began life as a 'msnusers' website on Bible Sunday 2003 with what I had ready for 'posting' - the Gospels, Acts and Revelation, Romans, a few more Letters and three or four papers. By New Year's Day 2004, the website had a complete record of my first summaries of the structures of all the Letters. The website was set up so that I could share my results with scholars, without delay. I notified many of my fellow members of the 2003 British New Testament Conference. It was a really thrilling time for me. I was very excited that my methodology was revealing all sorts of new things that I and no one else had ever seen before.

By March 2004, I had two-hundred copies printed of a pre-publication version of this booklet. Over a period of about four months I gave copies out free at Conferences in Sri Lanka, where I was serving as a UK Mission Partner. Other copies were sent through the post overseas and others were distributed by hand in the UK when I was home on furlough. All were given to people who I thought might give me some useful feedback. Honesty requires me to say that I had little response. Disappointingly also, I had few visitors to the website. (I have been aware for some time now that scholars and publishers have an aversion to anything new, especially when it runs counter to *many* 'currents and consensuses'.) I also kept trying publishers, but to no avail. Hence, I published *this* booklet myself: it was first launched in Jaffna on the 1st April 2005. It replaced the earlier website and pre-publication booklet.

Throughout the past year I have been able to revisit the results of my analyses, take another look, several new looks, and revise as I thought fit. I knew that revisions would be needed in the detail. There's just so much of it! It is a lesson I first learned with Mark. I know that still more sessions of analysis will better ensure a near 100% representation of what was in the minds of the writers as they wrote. How far am I now? I dare to estimate that I may be over 95% there.

A second edition of this booklet was prepared in July 2005, in the UK (after my return from five years of work with the Methodist Church in Sri Lanka). This revised edition was a stepping-stone to this new publication, which is accompanied by a disk of the New Testament Books in Greek, fully parsed and rhetorically analysed. It is only in the Greek, of course, that we find all the evidence that we need.

I am very much aware that this booklet and disk together represent only a stage in the process of recapturing for the Church all that there is to be known about its New Testament Books. My hope, therefore, is simply that many others will now engage in this work. Indeed, it is my prayer that this fresh perspective on the New Testament will inspire many new lines of useful enquiry.

I am a British Methodist Minister and Architect.

As an Architect, I am deeply impressed by the New Testament writers' devotion to discipline, in structure and style. As a Minister, I am convinced of the very real importance of knowing how each book is shaped, how it is structured, how it is to be described in all its parts and how the parts relate to each other. Book wholes are made up of parts. How else can preachers and teachers give themselves to exegesis and expository preaching unless they know 'their books' and know how each writer viewed the limits of the parts he presented and how he produced them to fit within his overall book, or letter format?

I am persuaded by my analysis and research that the writers of the New Testament were writers who possessed the skills of their era, writing to the rules of (what we now call) Ancient Rhetoric. Before anything was written down in its final form, each writer first gave great thought to the purpose of his work, his main ideas and how he would expose them, the plan of his exposition and how he would present it, and the style of writing which he would employ from beginning to end. Each writer was also aware of his responsibility to his first readers who will have had many of the skills that he possessed.

This booklet, I can promise you, will take you beyond your present understanding, whoever you are, New Testament scholar, or otherwise. Every page presents verifiable new evidence, new testimony to the skills of the New Testament writers and first readers.

David G. Palmer
June 2006, Wigston, England

Early Christian Literature: the Work of the Writers and First Readers

In this opening article we will explore first of all what there is to know about early Christian literature: how it came into being and the part it played in the development of Christianity as a new world religion. Then we will look at new evidence that will help us understand how this literature functioned and what was demanded of its writers and first readers.

Early Christian Literature

At the outset, we may acknowledge that the first transmissions of Christian belief and thought were oral, not written. The message of the faith was first preached. It was given verbally in answers to questions. It was debated. It was passed on, therefore, from the mouth of one to the ears of others. In the first decades of the Christian era, such an oral/aural method of communication was all that there was available to the church. And further to this, generally speaking, people did not read and write. Only a very few will have had an education based on reading and writing. Written communication was limited, therefore, to the privileged.

The period of oral transmission that both accompanied and followed the life and mission of Jesus Christ was an immensely fertile one. As people came to terms with what they believed was a new revelatory work of God through the life of one person, stories got told about him. Teachings which could be associated with him were recalled (and imagined?). And all kinds of ideas about him and about what he had done for humankind were entertained. This early, oral period of Christianity is characterized as fervently charismatic and enthusiastically evangelistic. The belief was that the Holy Spirit was at work.

Oral transmission, of course, continues today. But it can be said that, from the moment the church resorted to writing, Christianity embarked on a new and highly significant phase in its development as a new religion. This period was no less fertile than the earlier, oral-only period and stretched, in terms of the writings of the New Testament at least, from the beginning of the second half of the first century to the end of the first half of the second.

Given that the first writings appear to have been in the form of letters written by Paul in the 50's and 60's, we may judge that it was the spread of Christianity itself that led to their production. Paul resorted to writing to reach his dispersed congregations more frequently than he might otherwise have done if he had only visited them. And he needed to write, to make contact with them, of course, when he was in prison. Especially, however, the growing church needed written material to guide it in matters to do with its faith and its life. Paul understood this need and met it. (Others, later, added to his work: they wrote to guide the church in its organization of itself.)

A second phase in the church's first writing period, appears to have begun with Mark in the 70's. Traditionally, this gospel writing period is believed to have reined in what had been much based on 'eye-witness' and, supremely, on apostolic witness. It is commonly argued that as the first eyewitnesses and apostles were dying out, a written and lasting witness was needed. Another requirement of the church was of evangelistic material: the church had a mission to fulfil. It also needed its own New Covenant Literature as it came to terms with its separation from Judaism. Writings were needed which could be copied, dispersed, collected and read aloud in all the various centres of developing Christendom.

World events also had their influence on what was written and *when* it was written. Indeed, this second phase was likely prompted by one, supremely important event. For instance, nowhere in Paul's writings (of the first phase) do we read anything to do with the Fall of Jerusalem and the Destruction of its Temple. It is in the Synoptic Gospels only that we read interpretations of these cataclysmic events of 70AD. Initially, the church's assumption was that Judaism was finished and would disappear altogether. With the Gospel of John, however, we see how the church had to come to terms with a Judaism that was not finished, had not disappeared, but was surviving in a modified form. At the same time, and later than this too, we can see how the church had to cope with the fact of its own continuing existence. Explanation was needed for the unfulfilled return of Christ and the delay of the end of all things. The earliest literature (of the first phase of writing) had promised an early return and a judgement of all humanity. In the writings of Luke, in this second phase, we find him writing about the 'age' of the church. He thus filled the gap in the church's understanding of the divine plan.

(The embarrassing question, however, did not go away. An answer was needed. In the fourth and final phase of writing, as I describe it, it was penned. The 'Second Letter of Peter', written in about 145AD, provided the *acceptable* reason for the delay in Christ's return.)

Additionally, at this point we may say with good reason that each writing of the early Christian era benefited from the writings that preceded it. Indeed, in the first, Pauline, period of writing, we can see how Paul's own understanding developed with each letter that he wrote. He was inspired, we might say, as much by the pathways of thought that he continued to tread in a succession of letters, as by the responses he received from churches to which he had written earlier. A further, obvious point needs to be made. Paul's writings benefited more than anything else from the earlier writings that he knew so well, the writings of the religion in which he was instructed from childhood. Principally, Paul's work was that of making sense of the 'revelation' that was given him (Gal.1.11,12) in the light of the writings of the Old Covenant.

Though tradition associates Mark's Gospel with the reminiscenses of Peter, given the argument above for 'writing dependency' its association with Paul seems much more plausible. Paul's Letter to the Romans, 'Paul's Gospel' (tradition: Ro.16.25), is representative of but a step only away from Mark's Gospel. It tells of the eternal worth of belief in Jesus Christ, but very little about him and about what he taught. Mark's Gospel, however, tells of the 'beginning of the gospel of Jesus Christ' (Mk. 1.1) and as such it gives us a story, or a set of stories, about the man and his teaching and healing mission, his death and resurrection, *as well as* the eternal worth of belief in him.

Until Mark had written what he did, the church possessed no written down account at all of the life of Jesus. It only had Paul's writings and in them a few scattered details: Jesus' descent from David, his being declared Son of God at the time of his resurrection, the last supper, a betrayal, a cross, his death ('for our sins, *according to the scriptures*'), his resurrection three days later ('*according to the scriptures*'), the witnesses to the resurrection and a reference to a possible ascension (according to the scripture, Ps. 68.18).

The question becomes: Could Mark have gathered up, in the first instance, all the possible 'facts' that he could from Paul's writings and so begin his development of his presentation with these? The answer, of course, is, Yes, he could have. If this is what he did actually do, we would have to credit Mark with much more than he is usually credited! Someone, for instance, added 'day' and 'date' references to what Paul had established *according to the scriptures* about the death and resurrection of Jesus. It could well have been Mark himself (or more accurately: the one who wrote Mark's Gospel).

Of the very greatest significance in Mark's writing is his presentation of Days that for him began at the beginning of the twelve hours of daylight and ended after the four watches of the night. In telling about the Day of Jesus' crucifixion, Mark gives the timings of the significant moments as at the third hour, the sixth hour and the ninth hour, thus symmetrically dividing up the twelve-hour daylight period. In his telling of his last Day of his narrative, he begins the Day's account of the announcement of Jesus' resurrection with an introduction which is unique in the Gospel: 'And very early on the first day of the week... as the sun rose...'. Mark, therefore, gives his last report the fullest possible significance. The event at *the dawn* of the *first day of the new week after Passover* marked the 'beginning (of the announcing) of the good news of Jesus Christ (risen from the dead).'

My analysis of Mark's Gospel (structured as Four Series of Seven Days) demonstrates, to my satisfaction at least, that Mark's over-riding purpose was to show how Jesus fulfilled the requirements of the Old Covenant (in the first three days' telling of each seven day series) and how he, Jesus, established the New (in the final three days' telling of each seven day series). The Old Covenant was finished: the events of 70AD demonstrated that to Mark.

And these events, in fact, gave him his reason for writing. In the midst of *bad news* he had *Good News* to tell Jews and Gentiles alike. Mark was in total control of what he was doing. Tradition, oral or otherwise, most certainly had its influence upon him, but it did not control him. It is surely true also of the Old Testament writings: they influenced him enormously. But it was Mark (like Paul before him) who got to select and use them for *his* purposes.

Mark's Gospel, then, attempted the first 'description' of the beginnings of Christianity. It presented details (or what purported to be details) about Jesus' life, teaching, mission, death and resurrection. The Gospels of Matthew and Luke, in turn, attempted 'developments' of the same. The Acts of the Apostles, written in parallel to Luke's Gospel according to my analysis, presented a 'description' of the beginnings of the church and its growth in the Mediterranean world. Like the Gospels before it, the Acts combines soteriological and historiogaphical interests.

How then are we to view the purposes of Matthew and Luke? My analyses of their Gospels lend weight to the age-old interpretation that Matthew wrote for the Jews and that Luke wrote for Gentiles. I can see, therefore, no really good reason at all why we should date Matthew's work in the eighties and Luke's work in the nineties, as many scholars do. The productions of these two books could very quickly have followed that of Mark's Gospel. The primary dependency of Matthew and Luke on Mark is hardly disputed today. Their similar dependency on another source 'Q' is, however, increasingly challenged. To be rid of 'Q' we have only to make sense of Luke's use of Matthew. That is what Farrer said in the 1950's. My analysis of Luke's Gospel, I think, provides the necessary evidence. My analyses of the Gospels of both Matthew and Luke show that these two Gospels are structured in the same way. I deduce: Luke both knew and repeated Matthew's book-structure; his work exhibits dependency on both Mark and Matthew.

The writing of the Acts of the Apostles clearly belongs to this period too, though it is slightly later than Luke's Gospel. Signs of disjunction between Luke's ending of his Gospel and his beginning of the Acts - in the accounts of the dating of the ascension - suggest to me that Luke completed his first work before he ever thought about writing his second. When he did start writing again (encouraged by Theophilus?) he introduced changes in this ascension account. His immediate endeavour was to portray Jesus and his disciples against the backdrop of the Jewish Feast of Weeks, culminating in Pentecost. But essentially, before he began writing anything, he decided to create his second book as a parallel work to his first. (The two books are sectionally structured in the same way, both numerically and thematically, and details correspond section for section.)

What was Luke thinking? He was (surely?) intending to express the following: that just as Jesus had been brought to birth by the Spirit, that just as he had received his call from God and had been empowered by the Spirit and sustained in a life of mission through every kind of trial, so also the church was similarly brought to birth, called and empowered. The church itself, therefore, in its life of mission, would be sustained through every kind of trial, just as its Lord had been.

All these first four books of this writing period, then, represent something that is much more than just history. Each book has a specific overall purpose. Each book shows dependency, in some way, on those that were written before it. And yet, each book demonstrates a writer's freedom to re-write the details of 'events' and 'teachings', their sequence *and* their meaning. May we not say, therefore, that the writers' purposes were not primarily historiographical, but theological, Christological, soteriological and evangelistic?

Lastly, in terms of this second writing phase of the church, we may include John's Gospel. It need not have been written much later than Luke's Gospel. Its dependency on Luke and the earlier Gospels for some of its stories and details seems assured, particularly, in its presentation of a comparison between Jesus and John the Baptist at its opening, but also in its presentations of the clearing of the Temple, the feeding of the Five Thousand, the entry into Jerusalem and much of the Passion narrative.

(For an example of detail for which we can plot straight line developments from Paul, through Mark, through Matthew, through Luke to John, I think immediately of Jesus' betrayal at the hands of his betrayer, Judas Iscariot.)

John's originality, however, is not to be overlooked. Although we note similarities between Mark (for his use of 'sevens', his *Seven Day Series*) *and* Matthew (for his use of 'fourteens' in *'seven-seven'* arrangements of parts, in all but his balancing Sections 2 and 2') and John (for his *'seven book sections'*), we note this writer's greater presentational interest in 'sevens'. In his Gospel he has also seven feasts, seven signs and seven longer 'I am' sayings. John's Gospel also evidences a quantum leap in its Christology. Further, we can observe that it tells 'historical facts' differently. The book presents an overlap between the on-going work of John the Baptist and the beginning of Jesus' ministry (in contradiction to the earlier Gospels). It dates the clearing of the temple early in Jesus' ministry. It shows Jesus visiting Jerusalem several times (in contrast to the others). And it gives a different date for the Day of Jesus' Crucifixion. It is very tempting, of course, to view such differences as these as deliberate corrections of 'historical fact'. Rather, again, as with the earlier gospels, the differences are to do with the differences in the literary and theological purposes of the writers.

An interesting tradition (found in the Muratorian Canon) attaches to John's Gospel. But unlike the tradition that lends *historical veracity though Peter* to Mark's Gospel, this tradition affirms, through John and others, *a Spirit inspired veracity*. The book does look like it represents another imaginative stage in gospel development. Of the seven longer 'I am' sayings, for example, which liken Jesus to an interesting range of things, we discover that the first, 'the *Bread* of Life', sits opposite the last, 'the True *Vine*'. They are found in the balancing sections, 2 and 2' of the 1-3,C,3'-1' sectional scheme. The writer clearly intended something significant in this.

This second phase in the church's early writing era may be characterized as a highly creative, most fertile and imaginative one. Without it the newly establishing world faith would have been without its stories of its founder and the faith's beginnings and its stories of the beginnings of the church's mission in the world. Through the skills of the writers and encouragement from patrons and the church alike, the requirement of basic literature was met, was well met and diversely met. And the lessons learned in this phase got carried over into the next, the third writing phase.

It is in this third phase, according to my hypothesis, that some of the very best compositions of the New Testament were written. I include the Letter to the Hebrews, the First Letter of Peter and the First Letter of John. All three exhibit great skill in Greek composition. The Letter to the Hebrews, to me, is simply outstanding. This third phase in the church's first writing era, then, demonstrates the early church's capacity not only to continue with an exploration of the revelation it had been given, but also to produce the finest quality of literary work possible. It may be that without this phase the developing religion would still have established itself as a world faith, but it would have been without the writings that give breadth, depth and diversity to its understanding of the person of the Christ and its understanding of the church's calling.

Another book that was penned in this third phase is that of the Revelation to John. As a highly symbolic work, it reaches the peak in creative and imaginative writing, particularly for its numerology and coded messages. It further demonstrates the capacity of writers to be discovering new issues that needed addressing. In this book, the issue is that God is in control and all evil will one day be destroyed.

Lastly in this survey, we turn to what we might call the fourth and final phase of early writing. The third phase may have benefited from the second for more of the same earlier spark of creative and exploratory thinking, but the fourth did definitely not benefit in the same way from the third. It has to be said that the Pastoral Epistles and the Second Letter of Peter are on the defensive. The Pastorals have an interest in affirming teachings from the church's first phase of writing. And II Peter has an interest in promoting a reading of a particular gospel piece as pure history. One might say that these letters defend selected doctrine and demand simple, unquestioning belief. In these books, significantly, we have the two most important New Testament witnesses to the nature of the prophecies and writings of the 'Scriptures' (II Peter 1.20-21 and II Tim. 3.16). They are not thought up by men, but given by God. They are not to be questioned but believed. To these writers, such writings are certainly not the products of writers who were 'conscious literary artists, obeying conventions and imitating the correct models, like Hellenistic authors' (see Appendix 2, p. iii).

It is just possible that these later books display criticism of the kind of debates that the writings of the second phase spawned. These later books rail against 'myths'. (Are these the 'truths told in story form', as found in the Gospels?) One rails against claims that 'the resurrection has already taken place'. (Is this to be found in Matthew's Gospel, Mt. 27.51-53?) One impatiently warns, 'Avoid genealogies.' (The genealogies of Matthew and Luke do exhibit irreconcilable differences, but do reward close study of their schemes: *cf.* 3x14 and 11x7. Is the reference to these?) And lastly, while their common call for 'Godliness' and 'good works' is fine in itself, we might ask if it does not signal a kind of escapism? Is it not the case that the writings of the second phase simply posed too many uncomfortable questions for these later writers?

In ways, as above, we attempt, therefore, to sift the grand and the detailed purposes of early Christian literature, to discern the influence of world affairs upon them and the dependency of later writers upon earlier ones. As we do so, we interestingly discover the indelible mark of diversity, contradiction and tension in these writings. This writing period, in four phases, was clearly a time for exploration and experimentation in regard to all matters pertaining to the faith. It was also a time when all human skills and disciplines were offered to the divine task. Above all else it was a time when the human mind searched the mind of God with a passion. The unity of purpose lay in the conviction that Jesus the Christ and Son of God was *the* revelation of God in the world.

The writers, clearly, had purposes to fulfil for the church. But as we come to the end of this first section of this study, there is a point to be made, and made very clearly. It was not the audience that was to be reading what the writer actually wrote down. Between the audience and the writer stood another, a third party: the reader, or reciter. The writer wrote expressly, therefore, for him (her?). Only through the reader or reciter, and not through the texts alone, technically speaking, did what was in the mind of the writer reach the minds of his intended audience.

In short, the writer in the era of early Christianity had a responsibility to his audience for what he purposed to say to it, and also a responsibility to his reader/reciter who would deliver his presentation. The writing responsibility, therefore, was twofold: it had to meet its public requirement, but to do so, it first had to meet the requirements of the reader or the reciter.

The Work of the Writers and First Readers

We may speak of writers, readers and reciters, but before we do we need to define what we mean by all three.

Firstly, we consider the 'writers'. Most of the books and letters of the New Testament have the name of someone attached to them. We have names associated with each of the four Gospels, but they were later ascriptions (according to mid second century traditions) and unverifiable. We have the name of Paul attached to the majority of the Letters, but more times than we think it should. The names of companions of Paul attach too, sometimes a single name, sometimes two, but we don't know if they really contributed. Names are ascribed to other letters, such as Peter, James and John. But the First Epistle of Peter cannot possibly have come from the hand of an uneducated, illiterate fisherman. (This letter is one of the finest writings of the New Testament. Also, it doesn't look much like the work of a Jew.)

Interestingly, we do have the name of another writer. Tertius declares himself to be '*the one writing*' the Letter of Paul to the Romans (Ro. 16.22). He gives his own greetings 'in the Lord'. Elsewhere too, he or others (unnamed) are writing for Paul. When Paul does write in his own hand, towards the end of a letter, and also about the large (alphabetical) letters he is using, we are left to our own devices to interpret what this means: has he an eyesight problem, or is he unused to writing himself? We may rightly deduce that he always had others writing for him. We may be correct in thinking that others, named as responsible for the New Testament Books, had a writing practitioner working with (for?) them too.

The kind of picture that comes into focus is of (a minimum of) two, who collaborate in the same writing venture. One would be the one with the thoughts, ideas, or teachings to share (and the authority of the church to share them). The other would be the one facilitating his sharing of such things. He would be the rhetor: the one trained in 'writing', proven in his 'professional' skills in compositional method and in the fine art of writing. He is not an amanuensis (as scholars have long posited). He does not simply write down what is dictated to him. Rather, we may liken this rhetor to the modern day *ghost writer*, one who is employed by a busy celebrity figure unused to writing for the popular market. (The great and the good, and young footballers alike use them today.) Tertius, we may deduce, was Paul's ghost writer, in the writing of his Letter to the Church in Rome.

For the sake of moving on, in *the general case* we may name the New Testament 'writers' as the ones *for whom* works were written by rhetors. It raises interesting questions, of course. We have some letters written for Paul, but after his death, and one, at least, for Peter, written after his death (II Peter). We have Gospels with ascriptions that were later added. We have one purporting to be by John (understood to be 'the beloved disciple' of the Gospel), but completed after his death.

In *specific cases* there may have been churchmen who possessed *both* the thoughts to share *and* the skills to share them. Was the Letter to the Hebrews the product of such a person? Or was this the work of a rhetor employed by a *group* of leading churchmen? (Were *all* the Gospels produced in *this* way?) Or was the First Letter of John the product of one person? Questions abound!

In regard to 'readers' and 'reciters', what differentiated the reader from the reciter? They were both readers of course, but the reader, simply, was a reader only. Handed a Letter a short time before it was to be read in public, he would have read it quietly to himself to establish for himself its contents, structure, style and purpose. The reciter, however, would have required possession of a text, like a Gospel, a long time before he would have been expected to present it from memory, dramatically and convincingly. He would have needed time to read and to study the contents thoroughly and memorize them carefully. And he would have had to practise his delivery, before he recited it in a public place.

We may judge that the majority of the New Testament's Letters were written to be *read* out aloud (some *are* private), but with the Gospels and Acts in particular, we may easily imagine how their texts had been written for *recital*. With the exception only, perhaps, of Matthew's Gospel, they read like dramas.

The results of my rhetorical analysis and full parsing of the books of the New Testament do provide new evidence for assessing just what kind of literature it is that we are handling. It is clear to me that there is much more to the study of the Gospels and Acts than just their historiographical, evangelistic, Christological, soteriological and theological purposes. The manner of their literary composition, their structures, sub-structures and writing style (which evidence technical, even professional proficiency), would seem to suggest that these books were written to function in ways beyond those previously known.

When we see what we now can see, we need ask why the rhetor took so much trouble to exercise such great precision and care in the structuring and constructing of his work? It was not, surely, to satisfy the demands of ancient rhetoric for no real purpose? No, it was because the rhetor was writing for a reader or a reciter who would present his work. Conventions had to be followed, not for their own sake, but to enable the reader and the reciter to do their work.

It is all down to the text that the rhetor was to produce. I refer you to page 16 for an example of a fourth century text of columns of rows of (generally 12 to 14) letters, with no spaces between words. It compares with earlier texts like that of the Bodmer Papyrus (P75, 175-225?AD), a single column presentation of rows of (approx. 25) letters, with no spaces between words. The very first texts likely had formats of this kind. Thus, they all required interpretation. That the literature itself is styled and structured is to me indication that the rhetors wrote in the ways that they did to assist their readers with this interpretation.

There are four useful aids that the rhetor, under the rules of ancient rhetoric, prcvided his reader/reciter. He provided others, and they are all fascinating, but I judge that these four were the most useful. We look at them here:

i) In every one of the twenty-seven New Testament books, ***the ABB' style of writing*** is used, where A is the introductory piece; B is the first development and B' is the second and completing development. Indeed, in many instances Parts B and B' can be read as 'dualities'.

In all the books, these A, B and B' parts each break down into three parts, abb'. And each of these, in most New Testament texts, breaks down further into three parts, say .a.b.b'. In many texts each of these breaks down still further into three parts, represented, say, by (.a)(.b)(.b'). To the scholar or reader today of the New Testament who has never known this before, it will be considered an impossibility. But it isn't! It is certainly impressive, but the method can be learned and applied. I have personally prepared some sermons in this style. With practice, it *can be* mastered.

The reader/reciter, once he had discerned the writing style of the rhetor, would have been able to break down any text of unseparated letters into words, phrases, sentences, paragraphs and so on. He would have been able to define the beginnings, endings and extent, therefore, of all the writers' passages, just as the rhetor intended. The rhetor's writing style would also have assisted the reciter in setting the contents of a text to memory.

What is apparent in each New Testament book is that the rhetor, in his opening piece of his text, displays his style to his reader. Deliberately, it seems, the writer provided for the reader the simplest version of what will follow in his text. One of the best examples is in the opening of John's Gospel:

'In the beginning was the word	Aa(a)
and the word was with God	(b)
and the word was God.'	(b')

This is the opening piece, Aa, of the Prologue (1.1-18) which is completed with an additional two pieces, Ab and Ab'. It could not have been written more simply. The middle and final parts of the Prologue, parts B and B' (see page 27), display a complexity of the kind which the reader/reciter will encounter throughout the Gospel. In other words, this rhetor has made it his business to ease the reader/reciter into recognition of his book writing style.

The Prologue to John's Gospel is an ABB' structure. For comparison, the Prologue to Luke's Gospel is an abb'/abb' structure, a threefold *protasis*, followed by a threefold *apodosis*. Luke so begins his text, for the reader/reciter's sake, with a simple version of what will follow. As with the rhetor of John's Gospel, he is helpfully introducing *his* style. In the Acts of the Apostles, his second book, Luke presents a more complex abb', three-part, Prologue. Here, he appears to expect his reader/reciter to understand what he is doing (because he has read his first work already?). Mark, in his Gospel, also has an ABB' structured Prologue (see pages 18-20). It well displays *his* book writing style, as also the limits of the Prologue itself. The first readers/reciters will have understood this: subsequent readers, clearly, have not.

There is, of course, more to say about the writers' styles than just their three-part presentations. The New Testament writers demonstrate variety in the use of it. Though all the rhetors were trained in classical Greek and the art of rhetoric and had manuals available to help them (the products of instructors like Anaximenes, Aristotle and Cicero), some were either *able to write* better Greek than others, or they deliberately *chose not to write* in their best Greek. In this respect, and for an example, we might give a little consideration to Mark's style and method and his use of an unpolished, *koine* Greek. Did he lack skill? Or was it because he first wrote his Gospel in Aramaic? Others have judged, and I, that it was neither of these, but that he chose to write in a style that was appropriate to popular drama and for popular consumption. He 'dumbed' down his presentation, therefore, in order to reach as wide an audience as possible.

Lastly, on this matter of style, we ask: Where did this writing style originate? It is a fact that such a style is to be found in use in the writings of the Old Covenant literature. We find its use, for example, in Genesis and I and II Kings (for details of this, see my book, *The Markan Matrix...*, pp.24-25). It would appear, therefore, that Paul's writing practitioners were influenced in their choice by their Old Covenant predecessors. Subsequently, all rhetors were influenced.

ii) ***Anaphoras, anastrophes*** **and** ***inclusios*** are found in all of the twenty-seven New Testament books. They will have assisted the reader/reciter in his (her?) search for the sub-structures and structures of the texts.

Anaphoras are word or phrase repetitions which help define the openings of new sections or pieces in the texts. Once the readers begin to identify the rhetors' choices, the work of 'parsing' is made easier. Examples in the Letters include: 'Beloved' (see I John) and 'Brothers' (see I and II Thessalonians). The Gospel writers have their favourites: for Matthew, it is 'Then'; for John, 'These things..'.

Anastrophes ('hook words') are word repetitions that the rhetor includes, firstly, at the ending of a completed ABB' construction, and secondly, in the opening of the ensuing ABB' construction. They had a mnemonic function, acting as 'prompts' to the reciter, in two ways. As he completed one section, he was helped to remember the opening words of the section that followed. He was also helped to see that the two sections were significantly linked in the rhetor's thinking.

Inclusios are word repetitions which work at different scales/literary levels. By employing repetitions of a word at the beginning and the ending of a passage, the rhetor can establish, for the reader's/reciter's understanding, the full extent of one of his constructions. If the rhetor is defining a simple ABB' piece, then the key word or phrase will be found by the reader/reciter both in the Aa position and the B'b' position. Or if the rhetor is defining an ABB'/ABB' composite, or an ABB'/ABB'/ABB' composite (see Paul for much evidence of these), the same word or phrase will be found only in the first, Aa, piece and the last, B'b', piece, as underlined.

New Testament rhetors also begin and end whole works on similar details or themes. Inclusios can work at the grandest scale possible. Consider Luke's opening and closing pieces of his Gospel. His story begins in the Temple in Jerusalem (contrary to the stories of the other Gospel writers). It also ends in the Temple in Jerusalem (also contrary to the stories of the other Gospel writers). Similarly, the First Day's telling by Mark, of Jesus' night-time rising and temporary disappearance, has its parallel in his final Day's telling (the Twenty-eighth Day's telling) of Jesus' resurrection. Mark's Narrative begins and ends, therefore, on similar themes. Additionally, Mark's Prologue and Epilogue, which cradle his Narrative, exhibit balances of themes and details. These act like inclusios.

iii) ***A skeletal outline*** is found in each of the twenty-seven New Testament books. The rhetor was expected to have a book plan. The reader/reciter would be on the look out for it and would be content when he had found it. The writing rules required that it be a 'hidden' structure: if it was too obvious the work would be dull to listen to.

In Mark's Gospel, the narrative scheme (excluding for now the Prologue and Epilogue) is one of four times seven, Four Series of Seven Days, where there are two outer series and two inner series in the pattern: A,B,B',A'. Each Series of Seven Days is formed by an initial 'three-day' Sub-series, a turning point of a 'day' and a concluding 'three-day' Sub-series.

In Matthew's Gospel, the scheme is a chiasm of eleven sections, Sections 1-5,C,5'-1'. Each of these Sections comprises 14 parts, with the exceptions only of the balancing Sections 2 and 2' which both contain 14 parts, 10 parts and 14 parts (in an ICI', or ABA' arrangement). Matthew gives clear indication in his opening piece, Jesus' genealogy, that he is repeatedly using 'fourteens' in his presentation.

Luke's two works, his Gospel and the Acts, like Matthew's Gospel, are eleven section chiasms, Sections 1-5,C,5'-1'. In the Gospel, the same is used for the Genealogy, as also for the central teaching section. Luke's two books exhibit usage of sectional forms: ABB', AA' (or II') and ABA' (or ICI'). The latter breaks down, for example, as I(ABB'),C(ABB'),I'(ABB'). Luke never uses one form for one book-section, without using the same form for its parallel.

The Gospel of John is a seven times twelve chiasm, with Sections 1-3,C,3'-1' and with sections made up of twelve parts (abb';abb':abb';abb'). (We have noted above already the writer's interest in sevens).

The Revelation to John is a seven times seven chiasm, with Sections 1-3,C,3'-1' where all the sections comprise an introduction and seven parts.

The structures of all the books and letters are summarized on page 14 of this booklet.

Meanings clearly attach to book structures. The prime candidates for interpretation are Mark's 4x7 scheme, John's 7x12 scheme and the Revelation's 7x7 scheme. Numbers meant much to the early writers and audiences. '4' had its 'universal' significance; '7' was a sacred number in earlier religions, but to early Christians it signified 'completion', 'perfection' and 'fulfilment'; and '12' was related to 'God's elective purposes'. How do we interpret Mark, John and the Revelation? Mark: 'Jesus' fulfils God's universal purposes'? John: 'Jesus completes God's elective purposes'? The Revelation: 'All will come to its perfect completion'?

Another candidate for interpretation may be considered, but for different reasons. The structure of Paul's Letter to the Romans is a 1,2,C,2',1' section chiasm. The Old Covenant five books of the Law are arranged in the same way (I got this from a 1980's Jerusalem computer aided reading of the Hebrew and checked it out for myself). Did Paul and Tertius know its structure? If they did, then did they intend their audiences to make the connection? My analysis of the Letter affirms that 'the Law' is a significant issue in all the sections of Paul's and Tertius' composition. Aren't they saying 'Romans' is 'the New Law'? And isn't there something very similar to this in Matthew's writing? For he presents Jesus as 'the new Moses' and arranges *five* teaching blocks in chiasm, sections 2,4,C,4' and 2', interspersing them with other material.

Chiasms may have symbolic meaning. What we can say with certainty, nevertheless, is that they offered every advantage to the reciter. If he could remember his way into the centre, he could most certainly remember his way out from there. Essentially, chiasms *halve* the amount of structural information the reciter had to remember.

In the first and second centuries, both the reader and the reciter would have been looking in the text for the rhetors' book structures. As each took a manuscript into his hands for the first time, his first task would have been to separate columns of lines of letters into words and words into sentences and sentences into paragraphs and paragraphs into sections and so on. He would have been satisfied when he was able to discern the skeletal outline.

iv) ***Edentations*** are found in all our second to fourth century manuscripts of the twenty-seven New Testament Books. In the rhetors' *original documents* (*exemplars*), they will have added clarity to the presentations and been valuable visual aids for the readers' right readings of the texts.

Edentations vary a little in their presentation, but in all of them is a protrusion of a single letter or a half letter in the left hand margin of a presentation. Edentations behaved like the 'indentations' or 'indents' that we commonly employed to signal new paragraphs in our writings in the last century. For the reader, then, who had the rhetor's original document, these edentations were the clearest visual signifiers of his sectional and sub-sectional divisions.

In the laying down of the Greek letters in close juxtaposition, fourth century 'copyists' provided the relief of a *space* in the line above where the edentation appeared, towards the right hand margin of the column of letters. This space gave emphasis to the feature and the protruding letter was always the first letter of a new sentence and new paragraph (or section). Earlier copyists, of the second and third centuries, however, left no space before the edentation, but rather kept the rhythm of letters going in tight formation. The protruding letter in this case was simply the next letter to be written. The new paragraph, therefore, was begun in the line above it.

This earlier presentation of the edentation was flawed: it did not always show up clearly enough for it to be seen by the copyist. As a result, these signifiers of the rhetors' structures got corrupted, by loss as also by addition. We would have liked sight of even just one of the *exemplars* today, yes? But the next best thing, of course, is that we can now recreate them all, by examination of each text for evidence of the rhetor's writing style and structure.

It was the rhetor's job to facilitate the reader's work of preparation and presentation, and the reciter's work of preparation, memorizing and delivery. These four aids helped each one in his (her?) own distinctive task. And information about these things, of course, is information that we can use today. Indeed, it is vital for our reading of the New Testament Books. It is New Testament information that helps us define whole texts in terms of their parts and their wholes. It gives insight into the processes of their production. It also opens up to our gaze the purposes of the church's early succession of message bearers.

In moving to a conclusion of this part of our study, we may attempt further clarity on the churches' use of writers (rhetors), readers and reciters. It appears very likely that the church and its principal message bearers turned for help in the first place to those who had a practised and professional expertise. Rhetors were needed to do the writing and readers and reciters were needed to read and recite. But is it the case that only those who were educated in reading and writing were always used?

Literature played an important part in the establishment and growth of the Early Church. The need for communicators will have required that others became involved. Those educated in reading, writing and rhetoric, therefore, may well have been sent out to train others. Those so chosen, to be trained, would not have had to have had a formal education. They would only have had to be able to learn the contents of a manuscript, orally and accurately off by heart. Because oral education was effective and widespread throughout the Mediterranean world at that time, there would have been many likely candidates in the churches.

The Lesson for Today

A final and most important issue has to do with how the church came to lose sight of the internal characteristics of its New Testament texts and how it let slip through its fingers the expertise that was needed to do the texts justice. We have to entertain the possibility that this loss occurred early in the life of the church.

One possible cause for the loss is that the church's writing scholars were wiped out in the persecutions. Under Nero, according to tradition, leading, named apostles were put to death. Trials, executions and banishments took place under the ensuing emperors. Zero tolerance was shown to all those who were persistent in their profession of Christian faith. Known scholars, therefore, would have been very vulnerable.

A second possibility is that it was the *influence* of the church's writing scholars that was wiped out. Not the scholars themselves. In the first section of this article, we saw that the later writers contended with writers and readers of earlier periods: they wanted to commend texts for their historical factuality; they wanted to set aside debate and argument; and they wanted to affirm that the authorship and the authority of the texts were of God and not of man. Is the finger of blame, then, to be pointed at these later writers and not at emperors? Did this later group of writers gain the upper hand? Did they lead others to ignore any consideration of the rules of rhetoric, to which the books were written?

Tensions may well have existed between the writers, but what we observe is that they all did share the same writing discipline. It would appear that we cannot easily blame this later group of writers for the loss.

The third and most likely possibility has to do with 'language'. The missionary church needed translations of the Greek in the mother tongues of new converts (a manuscript exists from as early as the second century, in Syriac). The western church wanted Latin versions. And Augustine wrote, '...in the early days of the faith, no sooner did anyone gain possession of a Greek manuscript, and imagine himself to have any facility in both languages (however slight that may be), than he made bold to translate it' (*De Doctr. Christ.*, ii, II). The quality of the Latin varied. Different versions mushroomed. The fourth century project of the Latin Vulgate was born of this.

Is it simply the case that expertise in Greek was not widespread in the western church and that Latin translations did not replicate the internal characteristics of the Greek texts? (Because they could not? Or because no one tried? Or because no one realized there was anything to replicate?)

The lesson for today at least is clear, whatever the answers to all these questions. We need to be studying the Greek texts to regain both information and expertise that was lost centuries ago. All around the world today the church struggles to find a common path to the *truths* of the New Testament Books. As a result, it is intolerably divided in the ways it commends the living of 'the new life'. The supreme requirement has always been that of a purely literary analysis of the New Testament Books. In this booklet, I present, therefore, the results of my rhetorical analysis and full parsing of all twenty-seven books, as well as my own first explorations into the meanings of the findings. The disk provides the evidence.

PARSING:
What do *I mean* by parsing?

From the *Seventh Edition of the Concise Oxford Dictionary:*

parse *v.t.*
1) describe (word in context) in terms of grammar, stating inflexion, relation to sentence, etc.
2) resolve (sentence) into its component parts and describe them in terms of grammar.

I begin by saying that neither of the above definitions describes my work of 'parsing'. To me, definition 1) looks like an exercise for its own sake, and definition 2), though it is a little better, is one that I would want to re-couch.

I read 'parsing' essentially as 'part'-ing, by which I mean that the function of parsing is first and foremost the discerning of 'parts' and the *understanding* of them fully. But, of course, 'parts' can be defined only in terms of their relation to 'wholes'. The 'whole' has to be defined as well as the 'part'. Definition 2) appears to assume that we have defined a 'sentence' already, but if I read the definition correctly, that the use of the word 'sentence' is exemplary, it is not only the sentence, but also the whole paragraph, the 'chapter' and the whole book that have to be defined. In terms of the study of New Testament Greek manuscripts and texts, a 'book' is all that we can properly delineate first of all, not a chapter, or a paragraph, or even anything like all of the sentences. (Is there one verb or two or more in the sentence?)

The earliest New Testament manuscripts that we have display no sentences at all. They do not even display words as such, but only letters, some spaces and some edentations. (This you may have known before reading the preceding article.) If a New Testament scholar, therefore, accepts unquestioningly that the capital letters and full stops in the translation he/she is using are delineations of sentences *that the writer intended*, then he/she is accepting unquestioningly someone else's interpretation of the earliest manuscripts. I, for one, am not prepared to do that! Parsing of the New Testament texts, requires that, as part of the process, sentences, and paragraphs, etc., as well as the clauses that make up the sentences, have all to be defined, properly, from all the manuscripts and all the manuscripts' columns of letters (or as a short cut, from an up-to-date edition of the Greek text, *ignoring* all its punctuation, spaces and lines).

Given my experience of 'parsing' New Testament texts, the work of 'parsing' is begun with identifying a part, then another part, and so on, and establishing *only after that* what is the 'whole', the sum of the parts. This *appears* to be the opposite of Definition 2. The 'parsing' exercise goes on and on until all the 'wholes' that constitute the whole work are defined.

Now we come to my most important point of dissatisfaction with the definitions above. In the analysis of New Testament texts, parts are to be *known* not for their own sake, or to be *defined* only as an exercise in itself. Knowing and defining 'parts' is but one element of work in a much greater exercise. Satisfaction in 'parsing' comes not *with* defining a part 'in terms of grammar', but, *because* we can define it in terms of grammar, we can, therefore, *understand* the way each part functions within a whole. Ultimately, of course, we can then describe a whole text. And if we do the work correctly, we will all be able to describe it in exactly the *same way* as each other.

My particular area of work is about resolving *whole books* into their component parts. It is more than a work of 'parsing' only. My analytical method begins first of all with a reading of the text for its contents and its emphases. It continues with a search for any signifiers of structure. An exploration then follows into the writer's choice of style and his (her?) use of rhetorical conventions. It is after this stage that I 'parse' a whole text, *because* at this point, by close scrutiny of the grammar, I can *confirm* earlier proposed sectional divisions, or *resolve* difficulties. Parsing is a part of the process of analysing a text.

Given my particular usage, to 'parse' is to resolve any text into its component parts and describe them in the ways that they function (in terms of their content, grammar and position). It is parsing with a purpose and as such it is my modification of definition 2) above.

The Primary Results of a Full Parsing and Rhetorical Analysis of the Books of the New Testament

The Literature of the New Testament: Writing Style and Structures: An Introductory Summary

	Style:	Book/Letter Structure:	Sectional Structure:
Mark	abb'	(P) ABB'A' (E)	(ABB'XABB')
Matthew	abb'	1(p+);2;3;4;5;C;5';4';3';2';1'(+e)	(14s=2(abb'xabb')); 2 & 2': (14;10;14)
Luke	abb'	1(p+);2;3;4;5;C;5';4';3';2';1'(+e)	(ABA'); 1 & 1': (ABB')
Acts	abb'	1(p+);2;3;4;5;C;5';4';3';2';1'(+e)	(ABA'); 1 & 1': (AA')
John	abb'	1(p+);2;3;C;3';2';1'(+e)	(ABB';ABB':ABB';ABB')
Romans	abb'	(P+Intr.) 1;2;C;2';1' (E)	(ABB';ABB';ABB')
I Corinthians	abb'	(P) ABB';X;ABB' (N) (E)	(ABB':ABB')
II Corinthians	abb'	(P) ABB';X;ABB' (N) (E)	(ABB':ABB')
Galatians	abb'	(P) ABB'A' (E)	(ABB';ABB';ABB')
Ephesians	abb'	(P) ABB'A' (E)	(ABB';ABB';ABB')
Philippians	abb'	(P) 1;2;C;2';1' (E)	(ABB':ABB')
Colossians	abb'	(P) A:A' (E)	(ABB';ABB';ABB')
I Thessalonians	abb'	(P) A:A' (E)	(ABB';ABB';ABB')
II Thessalonians	abb'	(P) A:A' (E)	(ABB':ABB')
I Timothy	abb'	(P) 1;2;3;C;3';2';1' (E)	(ABB':ABB')
II Timothy	abb'	(P) ABB'A' (E)	(ABB')
Titus	abb'	(P) ABB' (N) (E)	(ABB':ABB')
Philemon	abb'	(P) ABB' (E)	(abb':abb')
Hebrews	abb'	1(p+);2;C;2';1'(+e)	(ABB':ABB')
James	abb'	(P) ABB'A'	(ABB';ABB';ABB')
I Peter	abb'	(P) ABB'A'(+e)	(ABB';ABB';ABB')
II Peter	abb'	(P) ABB'(+e)	(AA')
I John	abb'	ABB'A'	(ABB';ABB';ABB')
II John	abb'	(P) ABB' (E)	(abb')
III John	abb'	(P) ABB'A' (E)	(abb')
Jude	abb'	(P) ABB';X;ABB' (E)	(abb')
Revelation	abb'	(P) 1;2;3;C;3';2';1' (E)	(Intr., 1,2,3,4,5,6,7)

Notes:
Where 'A' generally signifies the presence of a lower level* ABB' *(or* abb'*) formation (likewise also* B, B' *and* X*); where* ABB' *(and* abb'*) are three-part progressions, where* A *is introductory,* B *is the first development and* B' *is the second and concluding development; where AA' denotes two abb' constructions in parallel; where 'X'/'x' is a central turning point; where* (P) *is an independent Prologue/Letter Introductory Greeting; where* (+Intr.) *is specifically an Introduction to the Theme of the work; where* (E) *is an independent Epilogue/Letter Closing Greeting; where* (p+) *and* (+e) *are, in turn, incorporated Prologues and Epilogues; and where* (N) *represents 'Notes of a Business or Personal kind'.*

**The exceptions on* A,B,B' and X above *are In Mark, Luke and Acts, where the sub-sections are variable composites of* ABB' *and* AA' *elements.*

Summaries of the Book/Letter Structures, their Sectional Structures and their Frequency of Use

Book/Letter Structures: seven types, in order of frequency of use

1st)	8x	ABB'A'	(one is a 'Book')
2nd)	4x	ABB'	(all are Letters)
3rd)	3x	1;2;3;4;5;C;5';4';3';2';1'	('Books' only, no Letters)
	3x	1;2;3;C;3';2';1'	(two are 'Books')
	3x	1;2;C;2';1'	(here and below, Letters only)
	3x	ABB';X;ABB'	
	3x	AA'	

Sectional Structures: seven types, in order of frequency of use

1st)	12x	ABB' (and ABB';ABB';ABB', which is sectionally ABB')
2nd)	9x	ABB':ABB' (and AA', which represents abb':abb')
3rd)	2x	ABA'
4th)	1x	ABB';ABB':ABB';ABB'
	1x	ABB';X;ABB'
	1x	Intr., 1,2,3,4,5,6,7
	1x	1,2,3,4,5,6,7:1,2,3,4,5,6,7 / abb'xabb': abb'xabb'

All the books demonstrate, to my satisfaction at least, that the New Testament writers employed the very same writing style as each other, of *abb'.*

Further, to me, all the books demonstrate the employment of book structure (seven types only) and book sectional structure (similarly, seven types in all). Eight books commonly employ one book structural form, four another, three another and so on. Twelve books commonly employ one sectional structural form, nine books another, two another, one another and so on.

I conclude firstly, therefore, that the writers knew the range of structures that were available to them. Secondly, I conclude that they were able also to identify the ones that other writers had used before them. Thirdly, it can be said of the writers that they were competent to choose the structures that they thought were best suited to their purposes: for presenting the contents they wanted to present; and for expressing, or adding, 'meaning' to what it was that they were wanting to say. Without doubt, the discovery of style and structure enhances our reading and interpretation of these books. We can now speak of their clarity and their aesthetic. We can also accurately discern their function, for the first time ever.

Given the fact that the New Testament comprises twenty-seven books, it has to be said that the book structures and sectional structures employed are remarkably few in number. Or put the other way about, the repetition of their use is really quite significant.

The presentations now follow of the primary results of my full parsing and rhetorical analysis of all twenty-seven books. Mark's Gospel is placed first, that of Matthew second, Luke's two books third and that of John fourth, in the order that they appear to have been written. The remaining books follow the usual sequence. I have not attempted here to place these in order of their production.

MARK'S GOSPEL

(For both Jews and Gentiles, a drama: Jesus completed the Old Covenant and established the New.)

Title: 1.1
Prologue: 1.2-20 (abb')

	Old Covenant...			Old.../New...	New Covenant...			
	A Day 1	**B** Day 2	**B'** Day 3	**X** Day 4	**A** Day 5	**B** Day 6	**B'** Day 7	
Series:								
1: **Jesus' First Days of Mission in Galilee and by its Sea** (172 verses)	1.21-38 AA'	1.39-45 abb'	2.1-22 AA'	2.23-3.6 AA'	3.7-4.41 AA':AA'	5.1-20 AA'	5.21-43 ABB'	**A**
2: **Days of Increase in Jesus' Mission** (119 verses)	6.1-29 AA':AA'	6.30-52 ABB'	6.53-7.23 ABB'	7.24-30 abb'	7.31-37 abb'	8.1-21 AA'	8.22-26 abb'	**B**
3: **The Days of Jesus' Journeying to the Cross and Glory** (112 verses)	8.27-9.1 ABB'	9.2-29 AA':AA'	9.30-50 ABB'	10.1-16 abb'	10.17-31 abb'	32-45 abb'	46-52 abb'	**B'**
4: **Jesus' Jerusalem Days, Passion and Resurrection** (239 verses)	11.1-11 AA'	11.12-19 abb'	11.20-13.37 ABB':ABB'	14.1-11 ABB'	14.12-72 ABB'	15.1-47 AA'	16.1-8 AA'	**A'**

Epilogue: 16.9-16,19,20a (abb')

Where A *is introductory,* B *is the first development and* B' *is the second and completing development of a three-part progression; and where X indicates a central turning point. Where, in the Series themselves,* 'A' *signifies the presence of a lower-level* abb' *formation (likewise also* a, B, b, B' & b'). *Mark demonstrates a numerical/numerological interest in a 'four times seven' scheme: 'Jesus fulfils God's universal purposes'.*

Below is a reduced image of the opening folio of Mark's Gospel in Codex Sinaiticus, AD331

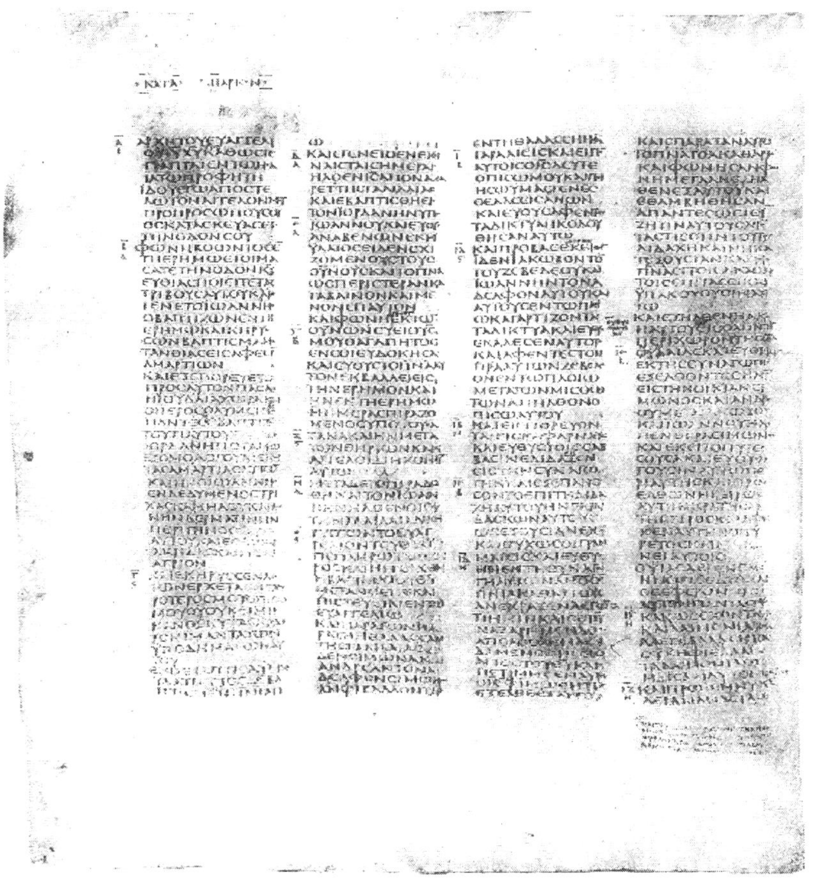

In this sample above, of an ancient manuscript, we can see how the Greek (capital) letters are in juxtaposition, without gaps between words, and how a space appears at the end of a line, followed, in the line below, by an *edentation* (the opposite of an indentation). We can be certain that this was an early method for signifying a break in the text, the beginning of a new paragraph or section of the book. Further, we may properly judge that these signifiers of sectional structure were fully present in the *exemplar*, the writer's original manuscript, but that these were omitted (*thoughtlessly*) or changed (*with much thought* – because of a doubt over the earlier version(s)) in the much repeated long-hand copying of the text, firstly from the original, subsequently from copies of the original and then from copies of copies.

An artwork of Mark's Gospel (supplied also on Disk)

Mark's Gospel is to be viewed as a matrix, which can be read both vertically and horizontally:

Vertically, for example:
In the two middle series, B and B' (in the art work: C1 and C1'):

compare the first days of each:	the issue is Jesus' identity: in both, he is John the Baptist, Elijah, one of the prophets;
compare the last days of each:	these are stories of the healings of blind people (the only two in the Gospel);
compare the middle days:	they both begin with common Greek words meaning: 'from there', 'rising up', 'into the region'.

In the two outer series, A and A' (1 and 1'):

compare the first days of each:	Jesus enters a city and the principal place of Jewish worship there;
compare the last days of each:	these are stories of resurrection (the only two in the Gospel);
compare the middle days:	they tell of plots against Jesus (the first and the last in the Gospel).

Horizontally, for example:
In the first Days of each three day sub-series (Days 1 and 5):
in the First Series we read about healings and casting out of demons
(the demons are ordered to be quiet);
in the Last Series we read about two disciples being sent by Jesus who foresees things.
In the second Days of each sub-series (Days 2 and 6):
in the First Series we read about individual men to whom Jesus ministered;
in the Second we read about desert banquets, of 5,000 in the first and 4,000 in the second;
in the Third we read about 'two' with Jesus in glory and, in turn, 'two' who wish to be with him in glory;
in the Fourth we read about the clearing of the temple of the old means of sacrifice and, in turn, about the new means of our being made right with God.

There are many more correspondences, of course, than these, of a straightforward Series to Series, Day to Day kind.
There are also *inclusios* in regard to the first and last Days of Series (e.g. the First Series: the healings of individual women and raisings from beds).
There are also *chiastic* correspondences (e.g. First Series Fifth Day and Last Series Third Day, and also First Series Third Day and Last Series Fifth day: for teaching content).

For examples of my parsing of Mark's text and of my attempts at a literal translation, see below (look out for *abb'* constructions, where *a* is introductory, *b* is the first development and *b'* is the second and concluding development)**:**

THE TITLE, 1.1:

Beginning of the (*tou*) Gospel (*euangeliou*)
of Jesus (*-ou*) Christ (*-ou*),
son (*-ou*) of God (*-ou*).

Or, possibly originally:
Beginning
of the (*tou*) Gospel (*euangeliou*)
of Jesus (*-ou*) Christ (*-ou*).

THE PROLOGUE, 1.2-20:

As it has been written A
in Isaiah
the prophet,
'Behold (*Idou*),
I send my (*-ou*) messenger before your (*-ou*) face (*-ou*),
who will prepare your way (*-ou*).
A voice of one crying in the desert,
"Prepare the way of the Lord (*-ou*),
make straight the paths of him (*-ou*).'"
There came to pass John,
baptising in the desert,
and proclaiming a baptism of repentance
for the forgiveness of sins.
And went out to him
all the Judaean country
and all the Jerusalemites.
And they were baptised by him
in the Jordan river,
confessing their sins.
And there was John,
clothed in camel hairs
and a leather belt
around his waist,
and eating
locusts
and wild honey.
And he proclaimed,
saying,

'There comes one stronger than I (*mou*),
after me (*mou*).
Of whom I am not fit,
kneeling,
to loosen the thong of his sandals:
I baptised you in water;
but he will baptise you in the Holy Spirit.'

And it came to pass in those days, B
came Jesus
from Nazareth
of Galilee
and he was baptised
in the Jordan
by John.
And immediately,
coming up,
out of the water,
he saw the heavens being opened,
and the Spirit
as a dove coming down into him,
and there was a voice out of the heavens,
'You are my beloved Son,
in you I am well pleased.'
And immediately
the Spirit throws him out
into the desert.
And he was in the desert
forty days,
tempted by Satan.
And he was with the wild animals,
and the angels ministered to him.

And after the imprisonment of John B'
came Jesus
into Galilee,
proclaiming the gospel of God,
and saying,
'The time has been fulfilled
and the kingdom of God has drawn near;
repent
and believe
in the gospel.'
And passing along beside the Sea of Galilee,
he saw Simon
and Andrew,
the brother of Simon,
casting into the sea,
for they were fishermen.
And he said to them, Jesus,
'Come after me,
and I will make you to become fishers of men.'
And immediately,
leaving the nets,
they followed him.
And going forward a little,
he saw James,
the son of Zebedee,
and John,
the brother of him,
and they
in the boat
mending the nets.

And immediately he called them.
And leaving their father Zebedee
in the boat
with the hired servants,
they went away
after him.

And the contentious, but likely,
ORIGINAL EPILOGUE: 16.9-16,19-20a:

And rising/ early/ on the first day of the week, A
he appeared first to Mary Magdalene,
from whom he had expelled seven demons.
That one (*ekeine*),
going,
reported
to those who had been with him
who were mourning and weeping.
And those (*kakeinoi*),
hearing that he lives and was seen by her,
disbelieved.

And after these things/ to two of them/ walking, B
he appeared in a different form
as they were going into the country.
And those (*kakeinoi*),
going away,
reported to the rest.
Neither those (*ekeinois*) they believed.

Last of all,/ to them sitting at table,/ to the eleven, B'
he appeared
and he reproached their disbelief
and their hardness of heart,
because the ones seeing him,
having been raised,
they did not believe.
And he said to them:
'Going into all the world,
proclaim the Gospel to all creation.
The one believing/ and being baptised/ will be saved.
The one disbelieving/ will be condemned.'
The Lord Jesus, therefore,
after speaking to them,
was taken up into heaven.
And he took his seat
at the right hand
of God (*theou*).
But those (*ekeinoi*),
going forth,
proclaimed everywhere (*pantachou*).

For my detailed arguments, refer to *The Markan Matrix...* (chapter 7). To the usual considerations, I add those of literary structural evidence, not only of the longer ending itself, but also of the form of the *whole* gospel. I add, not just in the chapter on the Epilogue, but elsewhere in my book, consideration of the practices of book and drama composition in the first centuries BC and AD. In regard to the usual considerations, I review the following: the issue of the *so-called* 'epilogue's absence from *reliable* early manuscripts'; the view that it 'does not square with the preceding passage, 16.1-8'; the argument over its 'difference in language'; the matter of 'dependency'; and whether or not 16.1-8 is the 'Epilogue', or that the Gospel never had an ending as such. It seems *to me* that none of the currently popular and scholarly arguments, for excluding *all* of 'the longer ending', stands up.

MATTHEW'S GOSPEL

(For Jews: Mark's Gospel, revised and extended, for use in teaching; Jesus is the founder of the New Covenant, as Moses was of the Old.)

Section 1: 1.1-4.24 Jesus' Genealogy, Birth and Early Years; His Baptism, Temptations and Purpose
(89 verses) 7:7 parts: 1.1-17,18-25,2.1-6,7-12,13-15,16-18,19-23 / 3.1-4,5-12,13-17,4.1-11,12-16,17-22,23-24

Section 2: 4.25-7.29 Teaching Collection 1: Blessings; the Law, Prophets, Religion, Coming Kingdom and Himself
(112) 14 parts: 4.25,5.1-2,3,4,5,6,7,8,9,10,11-12,13,14-16,17-20
5:5 parts: 5.21-26,27-32,33-37,38-42,43-48 / 6.1,2-4,5-6,7-15,16-18
14 parts: 6.19-21,22-23,24,25-34,7.1-2,3-5,6,7-8,9-11,12,13-14,15-20,21-27,**28-29**

Section 3: 8.1-9.35 Jesus' Galilean Ministry, His Person and Purpose
(69) 7:7 parts: 8.1-4,5-13,14-15,16-17,18-22,23-27,28-34 / 9.1-8,9-13,14-17,18-26,27-31,32-34,35

Section 4: 9.36-11.1 Teaching Collection 2: the Mission of the Twelve and Jesus' Mission Instructions
(46) 7:7 parts: 9.36-38,10.1-4,5-15,16,17-20,21-22,23 / 24-25,26-31,32-33,34-36,37-39,40-42,**11.1**

Section 5: 11.2-12.50 The Issue of Jesus' Identity: Positive and Negative Responses
(78) 7:7 parts: 11.2-6,7-15,16-19,20-24,25-30,12.1-8,9-14 / 15-21,22-30,31-32,33-37,38-42,43-45,46-50 (om.47)

Section C: 13.1-53 Teaching Collection 3: Parables of the Kingdom of Heaven
(53) 7:7 parts: 13.1-9,10-17,18-23,24-30,31-32,33,34-35 / 36-43,44,45-46,47-48,49-50,51-52,**53**

Section 5': 13.54-16.20 The Issue of Jesus' Identity: Positive and Negative Responses
(99) 7:7 parts:13.54-58,14.1-12,13-14,15-21,22-33,34-36,15.1-11/12-20,21-28,29-31,32-38,39-16.4(om.2b,3),5-12,13-20

Section 4': 16.21-19.1a Teaching Collection 4: the Church and Jesus' Instructions to His Disciples
(70.5) 7:7 parts: 16.21-23,24-28,17.1-8,9-13,14-18,19-21,22-23 / 24-27,18.1-6,7-9,10-14,15-20,21-35,**19.1a**

Section 3': 19.1b-21.17 Jesus' Judean Ministry (Journeying to Jerusalem), His Person & Purpose
(80.5) 7:7 parts: 19.1b-2,3-12,13-15,16-22,23-26,27-30, 20.1-16 / 17-19,20-24,25-28,29-34,21.1-9,10-11,12-17

Section 2': 21.18-26.2 Teaching Collection 5: Woes; the Law, Prophets, Religion, Coming Kingdom and Himself
(213) 7:7 parts: 21.18-19,20-22,23-27,28-31a,31b-32,33-41,42-43 / 45-46,22.1-10,11-14,15-22,23-33,34-40,41-46
10 parts: 23.1-12,13,15,16-22,23-24,25-26,27-28,29-32,33-36,37-39
7:7 parts: 24.1-2,3-8,9-14,15-22,23-28,29-31,32-35 / 36-41,42-44,45-51,25.1-13,14-30,31-46,**26.1-2**

Section 1': 26.3-28.20 Jesus' Celebration of the Passover, Betrayal and Trials; His Death and Resurrection; Disciples' Purpose
(159) 7:7 parts: 26.3-16,17-29,30-35,36-47,48-56,57-68,69-75 / 27.1-14,15-26,27-44,45-61,62-66, 28.1-10,11-20

The book is an eleven section chiasm, 1-5,C,5'-1', where all the sections comprise 14 pieces, but for Sections 2 and 2', the first and the last of the *five* 'teaching' sections, which each comprise 14, 10 and 14 pieces (many - smaller than elsewhere) in an ABA' chiastic arrangement. (The similarity of the endings to the five teaching blocks is noted. In the chart above, these verses are in bold.) Where the 14 pieces break down into seven:seven pieces, the arrangements of all the 'sevens', interestingly, are like those of Mark's 'sevens': abb'/x/abb'. (In the above chart, the middle pieces are underlined.)

Notes:

It will be observed that in the genealogy, his opening Gospel piece, Matthew employs a structure of three '14s' and so declares immediately his interest in '14s' and 'threes'. Reading Matthew, as with Mark before him, requires our exploration (like it, or not) into the meanings he attaches to his 'numbers'.

Though Matthew uses a numerical/numerological scheme to present his material, he does also employ the abb' *style of writing throughout.*

In the chart above, in Sections 5 and 5', I refer to verses and part verses which I omit (om.). In the Greek text, their presence in the original text is doubted. Parsing suggests their proper exclusion.

For book sectional structure, this book has to be compared with that of Luke's Gospel. This is a link between these two books that has not been observed before.

Here I present some samples of parsing in literal English from Matthew's Central Section, 13.1-53:

The opening piece *begins*:

On that day	a	A	Piece 1
leaving/ Jesus/ the house			
he sat beside the sea.			
And were assembled to him many *crowds*,	a'		
so that embarking in a boat he sat,			
and all the crowd on the shore stood.			
And he *spoke* to them		B	
many things in parables...			

Piece 7, 13.34-35, ends the first half of the presentation (compare the introduction to Piece 1, above):

All these *things spoke* Jesus — A — Piece 7
in parables
to the *crowds*.
And without *a parable* — B
nothing he spoke
to them.
So that was fulfilled the thing spoken by the prophet, — B'
saying,
'I will open/ *in parables*/ my mouth;
I will utter things hidden from the foundation.'

What follows, in the second half, in pieces 8-14, according to the writer, was for the disciples only, not for the crowds. Here, we pick up the content at piece 11, the central piece which, like the central piece of the first half (Piece 4), speaks parabolically of a 'separation' to come:

Again, like is the kingdom of the heavens — A — Piece 11
to a net cast into the sea
and of every kind gathering,
which when it was filled, — B
bringing it up to the shore
and sitting,
he collected the good into a container — B'
but threw the bad out.

Piece 12, the 'explanation' of 11, begins the last three pieces (compare Piece 8 which begins the first three pieces to this series of 'seven', for 'explanation of separation' and many words - common to both):

Thus it will be at the completion of the age: — A — Piece 12
Will go forth *the angels,* — B
and they will separate the evil men
from the midst of the righteous.
And they will throw them out into the furnace of fire; — B'
there,
will be the wailing
and the gnashing of teeth.

(And he says to them Jesus) — A — Piece 13
Did you understand all these things?
And they say to him, — B
Yes.
And he said to them, — B'
Therefore, every teacher of the law,
trained for the kingdom of the heavens,
like is a man,
a house-owner,
who brings out of his treasure store
new and old things

The writer (above, and significantly here) appears to be identifying *himself* and what it is that *he* is doing.

And it came to pass, — A — Piece 14
when Jesus ended*[1] these parables, — B
he moved on from there.*[2] — B'

*[1 & 2] These are two repeating 'conclusion formulae'. See the endings of Sections 2,4,4' and 2'.

LUKE'S GOSPEL

(For Gentiles: it is a fresh representation of the contents and meanings of Mark's and Matthew's Gospels, re-structured and re-mythologized. The presentation begins, turns and ends on activities – happening, or about to happen - in Jerusalem.)

Section 1: 1.1-80 Prologue; Angel's Announcements: Promises of Births;
(80 verses) **Belief and Disbelief; John the Baptist's Birth**
A(Prologue: aa')B(AA')B'(AA') 1.1-2/3-4; 5-25/26-38; 39-55/56-80

Section 2: 2.1-52 Jesus' Birth; Salvation
(52) I(ABB')C(ABA')I'(ABB') 2.1-20; 21-40; 41-52

Section 3: 3.1-4.44 Jesus' Baptism, Genealogy, Three Trials & Rejection
(82) I(ABA')C(ABA')I'(ABA') 3.1-20; 21-4.30; 31-44

Section 4: 5.1-8.21 'Sinners to Disciples'
(159) I(AA':AA')C(ABA')I'(AA':AA') 5.1-6.19; 20-49; 7.1-8.21

Section 5: 8.22-9.43a Jesus' Identity: 'the Christ', His 'Death',
(77.5) **Glorious Return *as Judge*, His Glory: Disciples' Purpose**
I(ABB')C(AA';AA')I'(ABB') 8.22-56; 9.1-22; 23-43a

Section C: 9.43b-19.48 Jesus' Journey to Jerusalem
(436.5) **(I) Setting Out; Fate of Jesus & Cities; 3 'Disciples'?**
I(ABB')C(ABA')I'(ABB') 9.43b-56; 57-62; 10.1-24
(C) His Teachings on 'the Way' 10.25-18.30 - - - - - - -
(I') Arriving; Fate of Jesus & Jerusalem; 3 'Servants'
I(ABB')C(ABA')I'(ABB') 18.31-19.10; 11-28; 29-48

1 Inheriting Eternal Life: Law and Love
ABB' 10.25-30a; 30b-37; 38-42
2 Prayer: Right Praying, Persistence, Holy Spirit is Given
ABB' 11.1-4; 5-8; 9-13
3 The Kingdom of God: what is Internal is Important
ABB' 11.14-36; 37-54; 12.1-12
4 Earthly/Heavenly Riches: the Coming of the Son of Man
ABB' 12.13-21; 22-34; 35-48
5 Divisions, Warning & Prudence, Repentance
ABB' 12.49-59; 13.1-5; 6-9
C Kingdom: Entry; <u>Jerusalem: Jesus is to be killed there</u>
I(ABB')C(<u>AA'</u>)I'(ABB') 13.10-30; **<u>13.31-33/34-35</u>**; 14.1-24
5' Divisions, Warning & Prudence, Repentance
ABB' 14.25-35; 15.1-10; 11-32
4' Earthly/Heavenly Riches: Coming Judgement
ABB' 16.1-15; 16-18; 19-31
3' The Kingdom of God: is Within, not Coming with Signs
ABB' 17.1-6; 7-19; 20-37
2' Prayer: Persistence, Right Praying, Receiving Kingdom
ABB' 18.1-8; 9-14; 15-17
1' Inheriting Eternal Life: Law and Love
ABB' 18.18-22; 23-27; 28-30

Section 5': 20.1-21.38 Jesus in the Temple: His 'Death', 'the Christ',
(85) **Return as *Judge* in Glory; Disciples' Purpose**
I(ABB')C(AA':AA')I'(ABB') 20.1-26;27-21.4;5-38

Section 4': 22.1-53 'Disciples to Sinners'; Jesus' Arrest
(51) I(AA':AA')C(ABA')I'(AA':AA') 22.1-23; 24-30; 31-53

Section 3': 22.54-23.25 Jesus' Three Trials & Denials/Rejections
(42) I(ABA')C(ABA')I'(ABA') 22.54-62; 63-23.12; 13-25

Section 2': 23.26-56 Jesus' Death; Salvation
(30) I(ABB')C(ABA')I'(ABB') 23.26-33; <u>34</u>-46; 47-56

Section 1': 24.1-53 Angels Announce, 'Jesus is Risen!';
(53) **Belief & Disbelief; a New Promise (of Jesus)**
A(AA')B(AA')B'(AA') 24.1-7/8-11; 13-27/28-35; 36-43/44-53

THE ACTS OF THE APOSTLES

(Luke tells that 'the Life of Jesus is lived again in the Life of the Church: it is a Life of Mission that the Spirit brings to birth, directs in the World and sustains through every kind of trial'. His scheme begins with activities in Jerusalem (and near by), turns on what happens from the new base of Antioch, both in Jerusalem and in Psidian Antioch, and ends in Rome.)

Section 1: 1.1-26 Prologue; Pre-Ascension Promises of the Spirit for Witnessing; Angels' Announcements;
(26 verses) **the Pre-Pentecost Days in Jerusalem; Judas' Replacement**
I(A(Prologue)BB')I'(ABB') 1.1-5/6-8/9-11 : 1.12-14/15-22/23-26

Section 2: 2.1-42 Pentecost; the Birth of the Church's Mission; the Spirit is given; All can be Saved, Three-thousand are!
(42) I(AA')C(ABB')I'(AA') 2.1-4/5-13 ; 2.14-21/22-28/29-36 ; 2.37-39/40-42

Section 3: 2.43-5.42 The Developing Church in Jerusalem: Arrests, Trials and Judgements
(110) I(ABB'A')C(abb'a')I'(ABB'A') 2.43-3.10/11-26/4.1-12/13-22 ; 4.23-31 ; 4.32-5.11/12-25/26-32/33-42

Section 4: 6.1-9.31 The Jerusalem Church: Stephen's Speech & Martyrdom; Persecution and Scattering; Saul's Conversion
(146) I(AA')C(ABB')I'(AA') 6.1-4/5-7 ; 6.8-8.1a/8.1b-40/9.1-25 ; 9.26-27/28-31

Section 5: 9.32-11.26 Peter, on Mission: the Role of Vision and the Spirit; Jesus is Judge
(86) I(ABB')C(ABB')I'(ABB') 9.32-43 ; 10.1-23/24-48/11.1-18 ; 11.19-26

Section C: 11.27-15.35 Three Journeys of Saul (Paul) and Barnabas, from Antioch:
(144) **(I) To Jerusalem and back (taking famine relief); James' Death; Peter's Escape;**
Saul & Barnabas deliver the relief
I(abb')C(ABB')I'(abb') 11.27-30 ; 12.1-9/10-15/16-20 ; 12.21-25
(C) On Mission, to Psidian Antioch, (Saul) Paul 'Turns to the Gentiles'
I(ABB') 13.1-3/4-7a/7b-12
C**(I(ABB')C(<u>AA'</u>)I'(ABB'))** 13.13-16a/16b-25/26-41 ; **<u>13.42-43/44-47</u>** ; 13.48-52/14.1-3/4-7
I'(ABB') 14.8-18/19-22/23-28
(I') To Jerusalem and back (over the Law and Gentiles); Peter's Speech; James' Proposal;
The Importance of Paul and Barnabas to the Church
I(abb')C(ABB')I'(abb') 15.1-5 ; 15.6-11/12-21/22-29 ; 15.30-35

Section 5': 15.36-18.23 Paul, on Mission: the Role of Vision and the Spirit; Jesus is Judge
(103) I(ABB')C(ABB')I'(ABB') 15.36-16.10 ; 16.11-40/17.1-15/17.16-34 ; 18.1-23

Section 4': 18.24-22.29 In Ephesus, Uproar; Sufferings Ahead for Paul; and in Jerusalem, Uproar and Paul's Arrest
(153) I(AA')C(ABB')I'(AA') 18.24-26/27-28 ; 19.1-41/ 20.1-38/21.1-22.21 ; 22.22-25/26-29

Section 3': 22.30-26.32 Paul's Trials: the Judgements and his Appeal to Caesar
(122) I(ABB'A')C(abb'a')I'(ABB'A') 22.30-23.11/12-22/23-35/24.1-21 ; 24.22-27 ; 25.1-12/13-22/23-26.23/24-32

Section 2': 27.1-28.15 Paul's Eventful Journey to Rome; All are to Die, but no, All are Saved!
(59) I(AA')C(ABB')I'(AA') 27.1-3/4-6 ; 27.7-17/18-38/39-28.6 ; 28.7-10/11-15

Section 1': 28.16-31 In Rome: Paul's Witnessing continues; Belief & Disbelief – Gentiles and Jews
(15) I(ABB')I'(ABB') 28.16/17-20/21-22 : 28.23-24/25-28/30-31

Where 'A' *signifies the presence of a lower-level* abb' *formation (likewise also* B & B'); *where* AA' *are parts in simple parallelism; where* ABA', ABB'A' *and* ICI' *are parts in chiasm (as* 1,2,3...C...3',2',1'); *and where* ABB' *and* abb' *are three-part progressions, where* A *is introductory,* B *is the first development and* B' *is the second and completing development (as also* a, b *and* b').

Notes:
In his 'genealogy', Luke employs a 1-5,C,5'-1' scheme of 7's; in his 'genealogy', as in his central sub-section, therefore, he (like Matthew) repeats elements of his overall Book scheme.
Common details are found between the book sections of Luke's Gospel and Acts: e.g. in the Central Sections of both books, at the centres: two 'sabbaths', 'eternal life', 'shaking the dust off... feet', 'entry into the kingdom', erchomeno (Lk. 13.33; Acts 13.44, both centres) and the 'Gentile Mission', prefigured in the Gospel, a 'reality' in Acts.
Luke (or his rhetor) is, without doubt, the Literary Artist of all the New Testament writers.

Below is a sample consideration of a section of Luke's Gospel, Section 4, 5.1-8.21:

Central to this Section is Luke's construction of a sermon: it is a three-part chiasm, ABA'. Each side of this central 'sermon' are four pairs of parts: hence the structure of Section 4 can be described by:

I(AA':AA');C(ABA');I'(AA':AA') *(see above for explanations of annotation).*

Sub-section I is **5.1-6.19**. The Section theme, **'From Sinners to Disciples',** in Simon's words, 'Depart from me, O Lord, for I am a *sinful* man', is introduced in 5.8, in the opening part, 5.1-11. The Sub-section focuses on **the fulfilling of the Law** as it progresses on the theme of what Jesus was doing for people (calling, healing, forgiving sins...).This sub-theme is introduced in 5.14, in the second of the two opening parts, 5.12-16.

The parts are: 5.1-11/12-16; 5.17-26/27-39; 6.1-5/6-11; 6.12-16/17-19

Sub-section I', 7.1-8.21, continues the theme **'From Sinners to Disciples'** in stories of what Jesus was doing for people. Its emphasis is on **the Prophets and Prophecy fulfilment**.

The parts are: 7.1-10/11-17; 7.18-23/24-35; 7.36-50*/8.1-3; 8.4-18/19-21

(*7.36-50, the story of the woman's anointing of Jesus: it may be noted that if Luke had not included this story here in his Section 4, he would most certainly have included it in his opposite Gospel Section 4'. The uncovering of Luke's structure acquaints us with the way his mind and pen were working on the pieces of gospel tradition that he was finding particularly in Mark, but also, I argue, in Matthew too. He does not fear to re-tell the story for his own literary purposes.)

It is in **the Central Sub-section C and essentially in the very middle of it** that the primary themes of the outer sub-sections meet: we find a comparison of **Sinners and Disciples** and, in the summary commandment of 6.31, a **fulfilling of the Law and the Prophets** (*according to Mt. 7.12*).

It is a carefully crafted Section, carefully crafted like all Luke's Sections. **Section 4** is well constructed with 'fours', 'twos' and 'eights'. It has not passed my attention that **Luke's Sections 3 and 3'** have 'threes' in their constructions (three 'testings' in the former, three 'trials' in the latter, and more). It is for reasons of this nature and all the above that I speak, in the notes attending the opening chart, of Luke's **'re-structuring and re-mythologising'** of the contents of Mark's and Matthew's Gospels.

Opposite, I present the central 'sermon' of **Section 4** in the New International Version, to show the **contents and form** of the sermon primarily. In parentheses I add words, from the Greek text that better express Luke's connections between pieces, and some capital letters. Even as he writes in 'fours' and 'eights', it can be seen in the Greek that Luke maintains his three-part presentational style throughout. For example, 6.31 literally translates: 'And as you wish/ that men may do to you/ do you to them likewise.'

Jesus' Sermon on the Plain (see 6.17), 6.20-49

[20] Looking at his disciples, he said: (A: THE PROPHETIC SECTION: 4 Blessings and Woes)

1 "Blessed are you who are *poor*, for yours is the kingdom of God.
2 Blessed are you who *hunger* now, for you will be satisfied.
3 Blessed are you who *weep* now, for you will laugh.
4 Blessed are you when *men hate you*, when they exclude you and insult you and reject your name as evil because of the Son of Man. Rejoice in that day and leap for joy, because great is your reward in heaven. *For that is how their fathers treated the prophets.*
1 But woe to you who are *rich*, for you have already received your comfort.
2 Woe to you who are *well fed* now, for you will go hungry.
3 Woe to you who *laugh* now, for you will mourn and weep.
4 Woe to you when all *men speak well of you, for that is how their fathers treated the* false *prophets.*

[27] "But I tell you who hear me: (B: THE PARAENETIC SECTION: 8 Commands; a Summary Command; and 8 Commands with Promises attached)

1 "*Love your enemies.*
2 (*D*)*o* good to those who hate you.
3 (B)less those who curse you.
4 (P)ray for those who ill-treat you.
5 If someone strikes you on one cheek, turn to him the other also.
6 If someone takes your cloak, do not stop him from taking your tunic.
7 *Give* to everyone who asks you.
8 (A)nd if anyone takes what belongs to you, do not demand it back.

1 "Do to others as you would have them do to you.
2 If you *love* those who love you, what credit is that to you?
Even 'sinners' love those who love them.
3 And if you *do good* to those who are good to you, what credit is that to you?
Even 'sinners' do that.
4 And if you *lend to* those from whom you expect repayment, what credit is that to you?
Even 'sinners' lend to 'sinners', expecting to be repaid in full.

1 "But *love your enemies.*
2 (And) *do* good to them.
3 (A)nd *lend to* them without expecting to get anything back. Then your reward will be great, and you will be sons of the Most High, because he is kind to the ungrateful and wicked.
4 Be merciful, just as your Father is merciful.
5 Do not judge, and you will not be judged.
6 Do not condemn, and you will not be condemned.
7 Forgive, and you will be forgiven.
8 *Give*, and it will be given to you. A good measure, pressed down, shaken together and running over, will be poured into your lap. For with the measure you use, it will be measured to you."

[39] He also told them a parable: (A': THE PARABOLIC SECTION: 4 Stories of Blessing and Woe)

1 "Can a blind man lead a blind man? Will they not both fall into a pit? A student is not above his teacher, but everyone who is fully trained will be like his teacher.

2 "(And) why do you look at the speck of sawdust in your brother's eye and pay no attention to the plank in your own eye? How can you say to your brother, 'Brother, let me take the speck out of your eye,' when you yourself fail to see the plank in your own eye? You hypocrite, first take the plank out of your eye, and then you will see clearly to remove the speck from your brother's eye.

1 "(For) no good tree bears bad fruit, nor does a bad tree bear good fruit. Each tree is recognised by its own fruit. People do not pick figs from thorn-bushes, or grapes from briers. The good man brings good things out of the good stored up in his heart, and the evil man brings evil things out of the evil stored up in his heart. For out of the overflow of his heart his mouth speaks.

2 "(And) why do you call me, 'Lord, Lord,' and do not do what I say? I will show you what he is like who comes to me and hears my words and puts them into practice. He is like a man, building a house, who dug down deep and laid the foundation on rock. When the flood came, the torrent struck that house but could not shake it, because it was well built. But the one who hears my words and does not put them into practice is like a man who built a house on the ground without a foundation. The moment the torrent struck that house, it collapsed and its destruction was complete." (NIV)

JOHN'S GOSPEL

For both Jews & Gentiles, the Gospel builds on the contents and meanings of the Synoptics. It includes: seven 'Signs', seven 'Feasts' and seven 'longer – I am' sayings. Jerusalem is much in the foreground, more so than in the other Gospels, as the writer rehearses issues that the church-in-formation was contending *with* Judaism from Jesus' time to his own, and *within itself* in regard to earlier Gospel contradictions. Jesus is fully God and fully Man. The structure is **a chiasm of 7 sections of 12 pieces (four threes, in two pairs)**. On page 11 is one suggestion of a *possible* interpretation of its 'meaning'. Here another is suggested. The Jewish *menorah* with its seven lamps in symmetry (to Jews, expressing the 'life and light of God') may have inspired the sectional structure. The '12' parts may reflect 'daylight hours' (see 11.9, just past 'half-way').

Section 1: 1.1-4.54 Integral Prologue; John the Baptist and Jesus; Peter...; Signs 1 & 2; Feasts 1 & 2: Marriage; Passover
(166verses) ABB'/ABB':ABB'/ABB' 1.1-18; 19-28; 29-34 / 35-42; 43-51; 2.1-11 : 2.12-22; 23-3.21; 22-36 / 4.1-26; 27-42; 43-54

Section 2: 5.1-6.71 Sign 3: Healing; Feast 3: 'a Jewish Feast'; sign 4: Feeding; Feast 4: Passover; 'I am the bread...'
(118) ABB'/ABB':ABB'/ABB' 5.1-9a; 9b-13; 14-18 / 19-30; 31-40; 41-47 : 6.1-15; 16-21; 22-34 / 35-51; 52-58; 59-71

Section 3: 7.1-9.41 Feast 5: Tabernacles; The Christ? Sign 5: Healing of blind man; 'I am the light of the world'
(153) ABB'/ABB':ABB'/ABB' 7.1-8; 9-13; 14-24 / 25-36; 37-52; 8.12-19 : 8.20-29; 30-47; 48-59 / 9.1-5; 6-21; 22-41

Section C: 10.1-11.54 'I am the door'/'the Good Shepherd'; Feast 6: Dedication; 'I am the resurrection..'; Sign 6: raising
(96) ABB'/ABB':ABB'/ABB' 10.1-5; 6-18; 19-21 / 22-33; 34-39; 40-42 : 11.1-10; 11-16; 17-27 / 28-42; 43-46; 47-54

Section 3': 11.55-14.31 Feast 7: Passover part 1; The Christ? 'I am the Way, the Truth...'; Parting Discourses, part 1
(122) ABB'/ABB':ABB'/ABB' 11.55-57; 12.1-11; 12-19 / 20-36a; 36b-40; 41-50 : 13.1-20; 21-30; 31-38 / 14.1-14; 15-24; 25-31

Section 2': 15.1-18.27 'I am the true vine'; Parting Discourses, part 2; Jesus' Betrayal, Prayers, Arrest & Before the High Priest
(113) ABB'/ABB':ABB'/ABB' 15.1-10; 11-16; 17-27 / 16.1-15; 16-24; 25-33 : 17.1-8; 9-19; 20-26 / 18.1-11; 12-18; 19-27

Section 1': 18.28-21.25 Feast: Passover, part 3; Sign 7: Jesus' Trials, Death, Burial, Resurrection & Appearances; Peter/John?
(111) ABB'/ABB':ABB'/ABB' 18.28-40; 19.1-11; 12-22 / 23-30; 31-37; 38-42 : 20.1-13; 14-29; 30-31 / 21.1-8; 9-19a; 19b-25

Where 'A' *signifies the presence of a lower-level* ABB' *or* abb' *formation: likewise also* B & B'.

Notes:

The above presentation records recent developments of what was published eighteen years ago in Sliced Bread... (1988). *This, my first book, explored the New Testament 'Books' for signifiers of 'structures'. My more recent research on Mark* (The Markan Matrix..., 1999) *led me into the study of the 'styles' of all the writers of these books. Rhetorical analysis, with reference to the first centuries' (BC & AD) rules of writing, makes clear the endeavours of the writers. And it is in 'parsing' a Greek text that a writer's employment of structure and style becomes very clear indeed. The result is that we can accurately define for the first time the beginnings and endings of the 'pieces' of the writers' compositions, and also the relationships between the 'pieces' that make up the 'wholes', which together constitute 'whole works'. The purposes of the writers (theologically, Christologically, etc.), therefore, also come into sharp focus.*

The Gospel of John compares, for structure and some detail (particularly for its use of 'sevens'), with the Revelation to John, but there is no relationship between these books as we find between the Gospel of Luke and the Acts. The sections between the books bear no comparison with each other; the writing styles are the same (as with all the New Testament Books), but the structuring of the sections is based on different approaches; and the purposes of the two books are wholly different from each other. The similarities seem to end with structural type alone.

In the eighty-third piece of the Gospel (21.9-19a), the number '153' (of large fish caught) appears. It is noted that '153'-'83'='70', the 'Gentile number'! It seems to me that the writer here affirms both his plan ('7'x'12') and his leading idea (the inevitability that the good news is rejected by Jews, but received by Gentiles).

It was a delight parsing John's Gospel. I am a convert! Previously, I thought the writing was 'laboured' and 'unnecessarily repetitive'. Now I see the rhetor's method, I see his purpose, the care he took, the intricacies of his approach, and the beauty of the book. The Prologue (like Mark's and Luke's) introduces the reader to the style and structure of the Greek that is going to be encountered in the rest of the text. It does not just introduce the book's key themes. Notably also, the rhetor uses 'Days' (*cf.* Mark), four of them, in his opening six pieces, to signal the sectional rhythm he is using. (For more in this booklet on John, see pages 54-56.)

Opposite is a sample of my parsing, in literal English, of John's Gospel: <u>1.1-18</u>, The Prologue:

In the beginning was the word A
and the word was with God
and the word was God.
This was in the beginning with God:
all things through him became,
and without him
not one thing became
that has become.
In him life was
and the life was the light,
and the light in the darkness shines
and the darkness has not overcome it.
There came a man B
sent from God
name to him John.
This came for a witness
that he might witness concerning the light
that all might believe through him.
He was not that light,
but that he might witness concerning the light.
It was the true light
that enlightens every man
coming into the world.
In the world he was
and the world through him became
and the world knew him not.
To his own he came
and his own did not receive him.
But as many as received him,
he gave to them authority to become children of God,
to the ones believing in his name:
who not of bloods,
nor of a will of flesh,
nor of a will of a husband,
but of God
they were born.
And the word became flesh B’
and he dwelt among us,
and we beheld his glory,
glory as of an only begotten from a father,
full of grace and truth.
John witnesses concerning him
and has cried out,
saying,
This was he whom I said,
The one coming after me
before me has become,
because first of me he was.
Because from his fulness
we all have received
and grace for grace:
because the law through Moses was given;
the grace and the truth through Jesus Christ became.
God no-one has ever seen:
(the) only begotten God,
the one being in the bosom of the father,
that one has made him known.

THE LETTER OF PAUL TO THE ROMANS

Writer: Tertius (16.22), following the 'methods' of First Century writing practice.

1.1-17 (abb': 1-7/8-12/**13**-17) Opening Greetings and **Introduction to the Theme**:

'The Righteousness of God and the Gospel of Salvation'

Section 1: (75 verses)		**1.18-3.31**	**All are Unrighteous, Under the Law or not;** **but God's Righteousness for All is in Jesus Christ**
(26)	**A**	1.18-23/24-32/2.1-11	God's wrath, man has no excuse; man's sins; he has no excuse
(26)	**B**	2.12-16/17-29/3.1-8	Apart from or under the law, all sin. For Jews...? For Jews...?
(23)	**B'**	3.9-18/19-26/27-31	Jews and Gentiles alike; a righteousness from God; a response
Section 2: (69 verses)		**4.1-6.23**	**Righteousness, through Faith and Grace, not the Law**
(25)	**A**	4.1-5/6-12/13-25	Abraham's righteousness; blessedness; by faith, by grace
(21)	**B**	5.1-5/6-11/12-21	Justified by faith, peace...; Christ died...; Adam and Christ
(23)	**B'**	6.1-7/8-14/15-23	Sin: so grace increases? Dead to sin. Not under law, but grace.
Section C: (64 verses)		**7.1-8.39**	**The Righteous Life, under the Law of the Spirit**
(25)	**A**	**7.1**-3/**4**-6/7-25	'...brothers', the law; '...brothers', died to the law; is the law sin?
(11)	**B**	8.1-4/5-8/9-11	No condemnation: the law of the Spirit; fixed on...; controlled by...
(28)	**B'**	**8.12**-17/18-27/28-39	'...brothers', by the Spirit; creation...., adopted sons; conquerors
Section 2': (90 verses)		**9.1-11.36**	**Israel's Rejection of Righteousness through Faith;** **Pursuing Righteousness still, through the Law**
(29)	**A**	9.1-13/14-18/19-29	Sorrow for Israel; but mercy for them; God chose this for them
(25)	**B**	9.30-33/**10.1**-13/14-21	Not for Jews? '...brothers', they did not submit; though they heard
(36)	**B'**	11.1-10/11-24/**25**-36	Not rejected; Gentiles grafted; 'Brothers...', Israel will be saved
Section 1': (91 verses)		**12.1-15.33**	**Righteous Living, in the Practice of the 'New Law Within'**
(28)	**A**	**12.1**-8/9-21/13.1-7	'...brothers', spiritual response; love and good; submit to authorities
(30)	**B**	13.8-14/14.1-12/13-23	Love, for the day is near; faith differences; do not judge
(33)	**B'**	15.1-13/**14**-21/22-33	Please neighbour; 'brothers...', Paul's service; Paul's travel plans

16.1-23 (abb': 16.1-10/11-16/**17**-23) Closing Greetings

Notes:

Where 'A' *signifies the presence of a lower level* ABB'/abb' *formation (likewise also* B *and* B'*); where* ABB' *is a three-part progression; where* 'A' *is introductory,* 'B' *is the first development and* 'B'' *is the second and completing development. All the 'parts' (1.1-7,8-12,13-17,18-23...) are abb' formations.*

Parsing and rhetorical analysis demonstrate that the text we have is one whole document basically in its original form (compare Second Century, 'shorter'/'shortened' versions): the only exception to this is that 16.25-27 (an abb' piece) appears to have been added later. It is neither supported by structural considerations, nor by the basic textual witnesses.

I write elsewhere in this booklet (on page 9) that I think it is possible that Paul was influenced, for his choice of structure, by the five-part chiasm of the Pentateuch. If so, this work represents 'the New Law'.

A Sample of my 'Parsing' of Paul's Letter to the Romans

(For 'arrangement', at first sight it could be any page out of the four Gospels and Acts.)

Ro. 3.19-26, a B part, taken from Section 1, sub-section B':

And we know	(A)	A
that whatever the law says		
to the ones under the law it speaks,		
in order that every mouth may be silenced	(B)	
and under judgement become		
all the world to God,		
because from works of law	(B')	
will not be justified all flesh before him		
for through law is full knowledge of sin.		
But now without law	(A)	B
a righteousness of God has been revealed,		
being witnessed by the law and the prophets		
and a righteousness of God	(B)	
through faith in Jesus Christ		
to all the ones believing		
for there is no difference,	(B')	
for all have sinned		
and fall short of the glory of God.		
Being justified freely by his grace	(A)	B'
through the redemption,		
the one in Christ Jesus,		
whom set forth God a propitiation,		
through faith in his blood,		
for a showing forth of his righteousness	(B)	
because of the passing by of previously committed sins		
in the forbearance of God,		
to the showing forth of his righteousness	(B')	
in the present time		
that he should be just		
and justifying the one with faith in Jesus.		

*Where **ABB'** is a three-part progression, where **A** is introductory, **B** is the first development and **B'** is the second and completing development. Important passage and book words are underlined, e.g. νόμου, 'law', linking parts **A** and **B**.*

I attach here a historical note, written on the 25th October 2003 as I finished my first parsing of any letter of Paul. It was a moment to savour!

Because Tertius is totally consistent in employing his 'three-part' style, it has been possible to delineate all his sections, sub-sections, parts... (I have done the job as accurately as I have been able in about 30 hours, but over many more hours I could get near enough 100% towards the writer's intentions). Knowing Tertius' method has made it possible even to 'parse' lists: see: 1.29-31; 12.6-21; 16.3-16. Personally, at this stage, I have analysed just over 70% of the New Testament (since completing work on Mark for my PhD). I am totally sincere in saying that long-'hidden' information in the texts themselves is available to us, through 'parsing' and rhetorical analysis. The clear advantage of knowing 'how' a writer has written what he has is that we can know, much more clearly than before, 'what' it is that he has written. We can now more usefully discuss also 'why' a writer has written what he has. Furthermore, we can now discern (e.g. as in Matthew) where later copyists added their 'bits'! The advantages are countless. A revolution in our reading and in our study of the New Testament is assured.

(Honesty requires me to write today, 9th March 2005, that I have just completed a major revision of my first findings!)

I CORINTHIANS (compare the Sectional Structures of Mark's Gospel: all as ABB'XABB')

	1.1-3	abb'	Opening Greetings	
A	**1.4-3.17**	**Lack of Unity in the Church; the Cross and Christ Crucified; Spiritual Matters:**		
	(61 verses)	A	1.4-9/**10/11**-13	Thankful...; '...brothers... divisions'; '...brothers...'
		B	1.14-17/18-23/24-25	Thankful...; message of the cross is foolishness...
		B'	1.**26**-27/28-29/30-31	'...brothers...', God has chosen the unwise/foolish
		A	2.**1**-5/6-7/8-10a	'...brothers', to know nothing except Christ crucified
		B	2.10b-11/12-13/14-16	the Spirit of God discloses truths
		B'	**3.1**-4/5-9/10-17	'...brothers', not spiritual, still worldly
B	**3.18-6.11**	**Church Practice: Apostolic advice; Sexual Immorality; Lawsuits:**		
	(51 verses)	A	3.18-23/4.1-4/5	wisdom, foolishness and judgement
		B	**4.6**-7/8-10/11-13	'...brothers', Paul compares himself... with them
		B'	**4.14**-15/16-17/18-21	'...my beloved children...': a warning: with a whip?
		A	5.1-2/3-5/6-8	sexual immorality: man to Satan
		B	5.9-10/11/12-13	written before, now writing: judgements
		B'	6.1-3/4-6/7-11	judgements, lawsuits among the brothers, shamed
B'	**6.12-8.13**	**Sexual Immorality/Foods; Church's Questions answered, in the light of the 'end':**		
	(62 verses)	A	6.12-14/15-18/19-20	your bodies are members of Christ; body/Spirit
		B	7.1-7/8-9/10-11	marrieds, unmarrieds and widows
		B'	7.12-16/17-19/20-23	the rest; remain as you are: circumcised and slave
		A	**7.24**/25-26/27-28	'...brothers', remain as you are; virgins; marrieds
		B	**7.29**-35/36-38/39-40	'...brothers', the time is short; virgins; widows
		B'	8.1-3/4-6/7-13	food sacrificed to idols, exercise of freedom
X	**9.1-11.1**	**Paul's Example: Rights and Freedoms, and Warnings from History:**		
	(61 verses)	A	9.1-2/3-6/7-11	'Am I not free...'
		B	9.12/13-14/15-18	Paul's rights, for the gospel
		B'	9.19-21/22-23/24-27	free, but a slave to no one, for the gospel
		A	**10.1**-5/6-10/11-13	'...brothers'; forefathers and God: a warning
		B	10.14-17/18-20a/20b-22	flee from idolatry
		B'	10.23-26/27-30/31-11.1	freedom and responsibilities, food sacrificed to idols
A	**11.2-12.31**	**Order in the Church and Lack of Unity; Teachings in Spiritual Matters:**		
	(64 verses)	A	**11.2**-7/8-12/13-16	'...(brothers)', praise for them, Christ, man and woman
		B	11.17-19/20-22c/22d-26	no praise..., divisions, the Lord's Supper tradition
		B'	11.27-29/30-32/**33**-34	Supper meaning, the body
		A	**12.1**-3/4-6/7-11	'...brothers', spiritual matters, manifestations
		B	12.12-13/14-16/17-19	the body, its members
		B'	12.20-23b/23c-26/27-31	the body of Christ
B	**13.1-14.40**	**The Excellent Way; Church Practice and Order, in Worship:**		
	(53 verses)	A	13.1-3/4-7/8-12	love
		B	13.13/14.1-4/5	spiritual gifts in practice: tongues and prophecy
		B'	**14.6**-12/13-17/18-19	'...brothers', speaking in tongues: its limitations
		A	**14.20**/21-22/23-25	'Brothers..', be mature; in church: tongues/prophesy
		B	**14.26**/27-28/29-33a	'...brothers', in church - Paul's guidance on order
		B'	14.33b-35/36-38/**39**-40	in church – women to be silent, order in summary
B'	**15.1-58**	**Death and Resurrection; Questions answered, in the light of the 'end':**		
	(58 verses)	A	**15.1**-2/3-8/9-11	'...brothers': tradition: Christ died, was buried, rose
		B	15.12-14/15/16-19	the resurrection of the dead
		B'	15.20-22/23-25/26-28	in Adam all die, in Christ... alive
		A	15.29-30/31-32/33-34	if there is no resurrection...
		B	15.35-41/42-44/45-49	how are the dead raised? With what body?
		B'	15.50-52/53-57/**58**	not flesh and blood...; do the Lord's work; '...brothers...'
	16.1-18	Business & Personal Matters		A (16.1-4/5-9/10-11) : A' (16.12/13-14/**15**-18)
	16.19-24	Closing Greetings 16.19/20-21/22-24		

II CORINTHIANS (structured exactly like I Corinthians)

	1.1-2	abb'	Opening Greetings	
A	**1.3-2.11** (29 verses)	**The God of Comfort; Paul's Hardships & Change of Plans:**		
		A	1.3-4/5-6/7	God's comfort
		B	**1.8**/9/10-11	'...brothers...': Paul's hardships
		B'	1.12/13-14a/14b-d	Paul's writing/their reading
		A	1.15-17/18-19/20-22	Paul's change of plans
		B	1.23-24/2.1-2/3-4	Paul explains, not 'Corinth': grief
		B'	2.5-7/8-9/10-11	grief, love and forgiveness
B	**2.12-4.12** (36 verses)	**Ministers of a New Covenant:**		
		A	2.12-13/14-16/17	Paul's movements and work
		B	3.1-2/3/4-6	ministers of a new covenant, in the Spirit
		B'	3.7-8/9-10/11	the glory of the new covenant
		A	3.12-13/14-16/17-18	hope, unveiled
		B	4.1-2/3-4/5-6	this ministry
		B'	4.7/8-10/11-12	treasure in jars of clay
B'	**4.13-5.21** (27 verses)	**The Spirit of Faith; Raised with Christ:**		
		A	4.13/14/15	The same Spirit of faith, believe and speak
		B	4.16/17/18	an eternal glory
		B'	5.1/2-3/4	a heavenly dwelling
		A	5.5/6-7/8-10	confidence
		B	5.11/12-13/14-15	living for him
		B'	5.16-17/18-19/20-21	in Christ: a new creation, righteousness
X	**6.1-7.16** (34 verses)	**Paul's Examples of Hardship and Joy:**		
		A	6.1-2/3-7b/7c-10	The grace of God, time and day, Paul's hardships
		B	6.11a-c/11d-12/13	'Corinthians': enlarge your hearts
		B'	6.14-16b/16c-18/7.1	Purity maintain: believers and unbelievers
		A	7.2-4/5-6/7	Paul's joy, comfort and boasting
		B	7.8-9c/9d-10/11	Paul's previous letter
		B'	7.12-13a/13b-14/15-16	Paul's previous letter: encouragement
A	**8.1-9.15** (39 verses)	**Paul urges Generosity and Boasts:**		
		A	**8.1**/2-4/5-7	'...brothers...': the Macedonian churches' example
		B	8.8-9/10-11/12-15	the example of Jesus, Paul's advice
		B'	8.16-17/18-21/22-24	regarding those being sent to you
		A	9.1-2/3-4/5	Paul's boasting to the Macedonians
		B	9.6/7-9/10-11	give generously
		B'	9.12/13/14-15	the result of your generosity
B	**10.1-11.15** (33 verses)	**Paul's Defence of his Ministry and Boasting:**		
		A	10.1/2-3/4-6	Paul: timid - face to face, bold - away
		B	10.7/8-10/11	belonging to Christ; absent or present
		B'	10.12-13/14-16/17-18	boasting in the Lord
		A	11.1-3/4a-c/4d-6	false apostles, super-apostles
		B	11.7-8/9/10-11	what Paul has been doing for them
		B'	11.12/13-14/15	what Paul will keep doing, compare false apostles
B'	**11.16-12.13** (31 verses)	**Paul's Boasting about his Sufferings and Vision:**		
		A	11.16/17-19/20-21	Paul boasts of his sufferings
		B	11.22/23-25/26-29	Paul compares himself with others
		B'	11.30/31/32-33	boasting in weakness
		A	12.1/2-4/5	Paul boasts of his vision
		B	12.6/7-9a/9b-10	Paul's 'thorn'
		B'	12.11a-c/11d-12/13	a fool, but an apostle (humour to end!)
	12.14-13.10	Business & Personal Matters		A (12.14-15/16-18/19-21) : A' (13.1-4/5-9/10)
	13.11-13	Closing Greetings **13.11**/12/13 (according to the Greek text verses)		

A Sample of Parsing: II Corinthians, from the Central Section, 6.1-7.16

In choosing the first two parts only, I am seeking to demonstrate how parsing discloses the discipline of the writer. We see how complex lists of similar details fall into structured presentations.

A 6.1-10

And working together — a — A
also we urge
not for no purpose
you to receive the grace of God,
for he says,
'In an acceptable time I heard you
And in a day of salvation I helped you.'
Behold now is the acceptable time. — b
Behold now is the day of salvation. — b'
No, — B
in nothing
giving cause for stumbling — (intro. to 1)
lest the ministry be blamed
but in everything
commending ourselves — (intro. to 2)
as ministers of God
in much endurance, *in afflictions, in hardships,* — 1 (*plurals*)
in distresses, in beatings, in imprisonments,
in riots, in labours, in watchings,
in fastings, in purity, in knowledge, — 2 (singles)
in long-suffering, in kindness, in Holy Spirit,
in sincere love, in a word of truth, in power of God.
Through the weapons of righteousness — B'
of the right hand
and of the left
through glory and dishonour,
through ill report and good report *
as deceivers and true men *
as being unknown and being well known
as dying and behold we live,
as being chastened and not being put to death,
as being grieved always, but rejoicing
as poor, but many enriching,
as nothing having and all things possessing.

B 6.11-13

The mouth of us has opened — A
to you,
Corinthians.
The heart of us has been enlarged: — B
you are not restrained in us
but you are restrained in your bowels.
But for the same in return, — B'
as to children I say,
Be you also enlarged.

Many of the Letters include a listing at some point. Because the writers are writing in 'threes', and in abb' style at the same time, we can, as at *, discern turning points in the writers' presentations. Here, as this writer completes a parallel, he is inspired to introduce his next six pieces in the same way, with an 'as'.

The following part **B' (6.14-7.1)** has been viewed by many as an insert. Contents-wise, it could be said to link with 6.1, if not with 6.11-13. It is, however, a necessary **B'** structural component in completing the first half of the writer's Central Section.

GALATIANS

My rough notes tell me that I first parsed this Letter in one and a half hours on the 27th November 2003. I said, when I presented my results then, that I reserved the right to make revisions on a future occasion. I do so now, even after further rhetorical and parsing considerations. Of the basic thirty-six pieces (3x3x4) about nineteen remain unaltered, but the structure itself is now viewed, not as an ABB' structure comprising ABB' breakdowns in AA'/AA' parts (36 in all), but as an ABB'A' primary structure with ABB' sub-divisions (still 36 parts in all: 4x3x3). **Paul is angry from the beginning!**

1.1-5 1.1-2a/2b/3-5 (all: abb') Introductory Greetings

1.6-2.10 **Section A** (29 verses) **No Other Gospel than the One Revealed to Paul to Preach to the Gentiles**

A	A	1.6	(abb')	***Paul is angry…*** : they are turning to a different gospel
	B	1.7-9	(//)	There is no other gospel; if one preaches another, let him be cursed
	B'	1.10		Paul in a quandary? No, he is a servant of Christ
B	A	1.11-12		'… brothers…', the gospel is not from man, but through revelation
	B	1.13-14		Paul speaks of his persecuting the Church and his life in Judaism
	B'	1.15-17		When he received the revelation, he did not go to Jerusalem
B'	A	1.18-20		'Then', after three years, he went to Jerusalem, to Cephas and met with James
	B	1.21-24		'Then', in Judea they heard of the persecutor turned preacher
	B'	2.1-10		'Then', after fourteen years, Jerusalem again: to uncircumcision; to circumcision

2.11-3.25 **Section B** (35 verses) **Not Righteous by Works of Law, but by Faith, Receiving the Promised Spirit**

A	A	2.11-14	(abb')	But when Cephas came to Antioch, Paul opposed him
	B	2.15-19c	(//)	Righteousness: not by works of the law; but by faith in Christ
	B'	2.19d(Gk)-21		'With Christ I have been crucified; if righteous through law, Christ died for nothing
B	A	3.1-5		'O foolish Galatians…'; by works of law - the Spirit received?
	B	3.6-9		'As Abraham believed God, it was reckoned to him for righteousness
	B'	3.10-14		Under the law/under a curse; by faith, promise of the Spirit; Abraham's blessing
B'	A	3.15-18		'Brothers…'; to Abraham a promise; the illustration of a Covenant
	B	3.19-22		'Why, therefore, the law?' By reason of transgression
	B'	3.23-25		Before faith came, we were guarded by the law; now, no longer under law

3.26-5.6 **Section B'** (41 verses) **Sons of God, Heirs, through the Spirit; Children of Promise; Freedom in Christ**

A	A	3.26-29	(abb')	Sons of God through faith in Christ Jesus; heirs acc. to promise
	B	4.1-5	(//)	'But I say…', sonship: heir and slave; adoption as sons
	B'	4.6-7		Because we are sons, God sent his Spirit; we are sons and heirs
B	A	4.8-11		Formerly, you were slaves, now also?
	B	4.12-18		Paul makes his appeal, 'become like me… brothers'
	B'	4.19-20		'My children…', Paul is perplexed about them
B'	A	4.21-27		'Tell me…?',; Abraham's two wives; two covenants/mountains: slave and free
	B	4.28-30		'But you, brothers…', children of promise, of the free woman
	B'	4.31-5.6		'So then, brothers…'; for freedom, set free; circumcision/un- is nothing

5.7-6.16 **Section A'** (36 verses) **Living the Life of a Free Person; Living in the Spirit; a New Creation**

A	A	5.7-10	(abb')	'You were running well, who hindered you…?' They will pay a penalty.
	B	5.11-12	(//)	'But I, brothers, if circumcision…?' The cross annulled? **Paul is very angry!**
	B'	5.13-15		'For you were called for freedom, brothers…'; the law's summary: love…
B	A	5.16-18		'Now I say, In the Spirit walk...', led by the Spirit, not under law
	B	5.19-21		The works of the sinful nature
	B'	5.22-26		The fruit of the Spirit
B'	A	6.1-6		'Brothers…', if anyone sins…; the responsibilities of each person
	B	6.7-10		'Do not be led astray…'; sowing and reaping; to do good to all
	B'	6.11-16		Paul's own hand..; circumcision/un- is nothing; rather 'a new creation'

6.17-18 (abb') Closing Statements and Blessing; Paul is still angry

EPHESIANS

The summary chart of all the New Testament book structures now shows that Ephesians uses the same primary structure as seven others and the same sectional structure as eleven others. Formerly viewed as an ABB' scheme of three sections with twelve parts per section, because of further rhetorical analysis it is now seen as an ABB'A' scheme of four sections with nine parts per section.

1.1-2 (abb') Introductory Greetings

1.3-2.10 **Section A** (31 verses) **Blessings; Thanksgiving; the Church; Alive with Christ**

A	A	1.3-6	(abb')	'...to the praise of (God's) glorious grace'; Father
	B	1.7-12	(//)	'...for the praise of his glory'; Son
	B'	1.13-14		'...to the praise of his glory'; Holy Spirit
B	A	1.15-16		Thanksgiving and prayers for their faith in the Lord Jesus
	B	1.17-19		Prayer that they will have the Spirit of wisdom, revelation and power
	B'	1.20-23		As exerted in raising Christ, exalting him and as Head of the church
B'	A	2.1-3		Former lives, dead in sins
	B	2.4-7		Now alive with Christ
	B'	2.8-10		By grace they are saved, for good works

2.11-3.21 **Section B** (33 verses) **In Christ: One New People; Paul's Preaching and Prayer**

A	A	2.11-13	(abb')	Formerly Gentiles, now near through the blood of Christ
	B	2.14-18	(//)	The two are now one
	B'	2.19-22		Fellow citizens; a dwelling in whom God lives through the Spirit
B	A	3.1-4		'For this reason.., I, Paul, the prisoner of Christ...', grace & revelation
	B	3.5-7		Revelation not made known till now, revealed to holy apostles
	B'	3.8-13		This grace to Paul
B'	A	3.14-17		'For this reason...' Paul prays...
	B	3.18-19		...that knowledge be given...
	B'	3.20-21		...a Benediction

4.1-5.20 **Section B'** (52 verses) **Live Worthily, Keeping the Unity of the Body of Christ**

A	A	4.1-6	(abb')	'...I, the prisoner in the Lord...'
	B	4.7-13	(//)	Grace to all, gifts to the church, to be built up, mature and in unity
	B'	4.14-16		Result: maturity, in the Head that is Christ
B	A	4.17-19		No longer live as the Gentiles do
	B	4.20-24		'.. not so learned Christ'; put off the old self, put on the new
	B'	4.25-32		Speak truth; give no room to the devil; don't grieve the Spirit
B'	A	5.1-5		Walk in love; among you, no hint of sexual immorality; no such person inherits...
	B	5.6-14		Do not be deceived, you were in darkness, but now you are light
	B'	5.15-20		Be wise how you live

5.21-6.20 **Section A'** (33 verses) **Christ-centred Relationships: Christ and the Church**

A	A	5.21-24	(abb')	Submit to one another; Wives...
	B	5.25-27	(//)	Husbands love your wives...
	B'	5.28-30		So ought Husbands to love their wives...
B	A	5.31-33		The mystery of two becoming one and Christ and his Church
	B	6.1-4		Children and Fathers
	B'	6.5-9		Slaves and Masters, ...Lord
B'	A	6.10-12		'Finally...' 'be strong in the Lord...'; 'put on the full armour of God...'
	B	6.13-17		'...put on the full armour of God...'
	B'	6.18-20		'Pray in the Spirit...', watching and praying

6.21-24 (abb') Closing Statements and Blessing (21/22/23-24)

Notes:

This letter's compositional method exhibits well a 'chain link' presentation, whereby inter- and intra-sectional link words and subjects are established at the endings of parts and at the beginnings of the following parts. It was one suggestion for a writing rule and method in Ancient Rhetoric (as expressed by Lucian in the 160's AD, because it was in general use before he wrote his manual).

PHILIPPIANS

The Structure of the letter is a five section chiasm, similar to that of Romans and Hebrews, where the sections are constructed as ABB':ABB', like I & II Corinthians, II Thessalonians, I Timothy, Titus, Philemon, Hebrews and II Peter. Each part further comprises three parts, abb'.

1.1-2	(abb')	Introductory Greetings: from Paul and Timothy...; to the saints...; grace and peace... from the Lord Jesus Christ			
1.3-20		**Section 1** (18 verses)			**Thanksgiving and Prayer; Rejoicing, though in chains**
	A	A	1.3-5	(abb')	'I thank my God...'; with joy, petition, for fellowship in the gospel
		B	1.6-8	(abb')	Confident of completion by the day of Christ Jesus; they are in his heart
		B'	1.9-11	(//)	He prays for them: for the fruit of righteousness through Jesus Christ
	A'	A	1.12-14		'...brothers...' Paul's chains; advance of the gospel, speaking the word of God
		B	1.15-17		Proclaiming Christ with different motives; some to make trouble for Paul
		B'	1.18-20		'What then?... Christ is preached...'; Paul' salvation, whether life or death
1.21-2.11		**Section 2** (21 verses)			**Oriented Heavenwards in Ministry and in the Church**
	A	A	1.21-26	(//)	'For me to live is Christ and to die is gain', but which of the two?
		B	1.27		Worthy of the gospel of Christ, in one spirit, with one soul
		B'	1.28-30		Terrified of nothing; believing and suffering; as Paul
	A'	A	2.1-2		'If there be any comfort in Christ...': think the same, have the same love...
		B	2.3-4		No rivalry, in humility each one looking out for the other
		B'	2.5-11		Think on Christ Jesus, he made himself nothing..., and God exalted him
2.12-30		**Section C** (19 verses)			**Rejoices in his Ministry; sends Timothy and Epaphroditus**
	A	A	2.12-13	(//)	'So, my beloved...', work out your salvation, be blameless and faultless
		B	2.14-18		Faultless children of God, shining in the world, whatever happens to Paul
		B'	2.19-22		Paul hopes to send Timothy to them soon; he is commended to them
	A'	A	2.23-24		'This one... I hope to send...'; but Paul himself hopes to come shortly
		B	2.25-27		Necessarily, he returns Epaphroditus to them: he was longing for them
		B'	2.28-30		He is sent back so they may rejoice; he almost died for the work of Christ
3.1-21		**Section 2'** (21 verses)			**Oriented Heavenwards, Rejoice in the Lord**
	A	A	3.1-6	(//)	'For the rest, my brothers, rejoice in the Lord..'; true circumcision
		B	3.7-9a		Loss for the sake of Christ and the gain of knowing Christ
		B'	3.9b-12		Righteous through faith in Christ; to know and to attain to the resurrection
	A'	A	3.13-16		'Brothers...'; pressing on for the prize of the high calling of God in Christ Jesus
		B	3.17-19		'Be imitators of me, brothers'; others glory in their shame, their earthly thinking
		B'	3.20-21		'For our citizenship is in Heaven, from where we await also a Saviour
4.1-20		**Section 1'** (20 verses)			**Stand and Rejoice in the Lord; Paul's Needs and their Needs**
	A	A	4.1-3	(//)	'So, my brothers... stand in the Lord, beloved'; beseechings, think the same
		B	4.4-7		'Rejoice in the Lord always...', 'the peace of God'
		B'	4.8-9		'For the rest, brothers, whatever things are true... the God of peace...'
	A'	A	4.10-14		Paul rejoices greatly in the Lord for their concern for his needs
		B	4.15-17		they met his needs in Thessalonica; he seeks credit for them
		B'	4.18-20		He is amply supplied, through Epaphroditus; God will meet their needs
4.21-23	(abb')	Closing Greetings: Greet every saint...; all the saints greet...; the grace of the Lord Jesus Christ...			

Notes (as produced for the first publication of this booklet):
I am aware that this summary and all like it are not wholly adequate vehicles for the presentation of the New Testament's Book and Letter structures, but for the moment they will have to suffice. The publishing task of producing the Greek Texts in their entirety will be a bigger challenge than producing this booklet and not exactly what a lot of readers will want. At least it can be seen from the above information that this letter exhibits good balance and linkage, but I'm still looking at the overall structure, to see if there is a better way of describing it, though the content repetitions of 2.19-22/23-24 do suggest a 'centre'.

COLOSSIANS

The Structure of this letter is a simple **A:A'** form, where each whole section comprises sub-sections ABB'. Each of these further breaks down into three parts, ABB', and each of these breaks down into another three parts, abb'. See IThessalonians for use of the same 'letter' structure and the same sectional structure.

1.1-2	(abb')	Introductory Greetings: from Paul and Timothy...; to the saints...; grace and peace... from God our Father			
1.3-2.19		**Composite Section A: Thanks, Prayers and Affirmations** (46 verses)			
A (18 verses)		A	1.3-8	(abb')	Thanks, praying:
		B	1.9-14	(//)	Praying; the kingdom of the Son
		B'	1.15-20		Supremacy of the Son: 'the Head' of the church; reconciling
B (14 verses)		A	1.21-23		Once alienated, now reconciled
		B	1.24-29		Paul rejoices in sufferings; commission to Gentiles; mystery; struggling
		B'	2.1-5		Paul's struggles, purpose; Laodicea; mystery
B' (14 verses)		A	2.6-10		As you received Christ, 'walk' in him, 'the Head' of all rule and authority
		B	2.11-15		Circumcised... of Christ; co-buried with him; made alive with him
		B'	2.16-19		Do not be judged or misled; the reality is Christ, 'the Head'
2.20-4.17		**Composite Section A': The Old Life and The New Life** (46 verses)			
A (15 verses)		A	2.20-23	(//)	If you died with Christ...; why live under the world's rules?
		B	3.1-4		If, therefore, you were co-raised with Christ...; things above; glory
		B'	3.5-11		Put to death, therefore...; but now put away...
B (15verses)		A	3.12-14		Put on, therefore...; live the new life
		B	3.15-17		New life in the peace and word of Christ, being thankful
		B'	3.18-4.1		New rules for Christian Households
B' (16 verses)		A	4.2-6		Devote to prayer, walk in wisdom, know how to answer
		B	4.7-9		Tychicus will give news; giving comfort; and so too Onesimus
		B'	4.10-17		Greetings, from... and to..., and instructions
4.18	(abb')	Paul's Closing Greetings in his own hand			

Notes:
Up until the 3rd February 2005, I viewed the letter's structure in two halves (1.3-2.15 and 2.16-4.6) with a separate, extra piece of 4.7-18. I viewed each section as comprising A(A(AA')A'(AA'))A'(A(AA')A'(AA')) parts, where the eight parts shown, in pairs as (AA'), broke down further into abb' parts. A review led to the above which, to my mind, now fully satisfies the criteria for ABB' arrangements, whereby A is the opening part, B is the first development and B' is the second and concluding development.

Below is the parsed text of the Introductory Greetings

1.1-2
Paul
    apostle of Christ Jesus — a
        through the will of God
    and Timothy
        the brother.
To the saints in Colossae — b
    and faithful brothers
    in Christ.
Grace to you — b'
    and peace
    from God our father.

My rough notes tell me that **I and II Thessalonians** were first parsed on the 21st November 2003 and that the latter was initially parsed in only half an hour. I Thessalonians took longer because it was the first of the two to be parsed (lessons had to be learned) and because it *is* longer! It will be seen below that the two letters have a similar overall structure, but that the first employs ABB';ABB';ABB' for a sectional structure and that the second employs the simpler and shorter form of ABB':ABB'.

I THESSALONIANS

The structure of this letter is a simple **A:A'** form, where each whole section comprises sub-sections ABB'. Each of these further breaks down into three parts, ABB', and each of these breaks down further into abb' parts.

1.1 (abb') Introductory Greetings: from Paul, Silas and Timothy; to the church...; grace and peace...

1.2-3.13 **Composite Section A** (42 verses)

A (17 verses)	A	1.2-3	(abb')	Thanks to God for them and prayers
	B	1.4-10	(//)	'Knowing, brothers, beloved...', their 'way in', *εἴσοδον*
	B'	2.1-8		'For... brothers...', their 'way in', *εἴσοδον*
B (12 verses)	A	2.9-13		'For... brothers...', their labour and example
	B	2.14-16		'For imitators you became, brothers, of the churches...'
	B'	2.17-20		'But we brothers...', wanted to come
B' (13 verses)	A	3.1-6		In Athens, they sent Timothy to them
	B	3.7-10		'Therefore, we were comforted, brothers...',
	B'	3.11-13		Now God, Father, Jesus... direct our 'way' to you

4.1-5.27 **Composite Section A'** (45 verses)

A (12 verses)	A	4.1-2	(//)	'For the rest, therefore, brothers... so walk' rightly
	B	4.3-8		'For this is the will of God...': their sanctification
	B'	4.9-12		'...brotherly love.... brothers'; love one another, walk rightly
B (17 verses)	A	4.13-18		'Now... not to be ignorant, brothers...', the coming of the Lord
	B	5.1-3		'Now... times and seasons, brothers...'; as a thief at night
	B'	5.4-11		'But you brothers...', as sons of light, be alert
B' (16 verses)	A	5.12-13		'Now we ask you, brothers...' consider your leaders
	B	5.14-24		'And we exhort you, brothers...', don't pay back wrong...
	B'	5.25-27		'Brothers, pray - concerning us'; greetings; regarding the letter

5.28 (abb') Closing Grace

Below is another example of parsing, in literal English: the Opening Greetings to this letter. It compares with the Greetings in the second letter:

1.1
Paul — a
and Silvanus
and Timothy,
to the church of Thessalonians — b
in Father God
and Lord Jesus Christ,
grace to you — b'
and peace.

II THESSALONIANS

The structure of this letter is a simple **A:A'** form, where each whole section comprises sub-sections A:A'. Each of these breaks down further into three parts, ABB', and each of these, further, into abb' parts.

1.1-2 (abb') Introductory Greetings: from Paul, Silas and Timothy; to the church...; grace and peace...

1.3-2.12 **Composite Section A** (22 verses)

A (10 verses)	A	1.3-5 (abb')	Thanks to God always*, 'brothers', their faith is growing
	B	1.6-10 (abb')	God is just, he will pay back/give relief when he comes
	B'	1.11-12 (//)	They are praying that they may be worthy of their calling
A' (12 verses)	A	2.1-4	'...brothers': Concerning the coming: don't be deceived
	B	2.5-7	Remember what Paul said about the mystery of lawlessness
	B'	2.8-12	The coming of the lawless one; all deluded - condemned

2.13-3.16c **Composite Section A'** (20 ¾ verses)

A (10 verses)	A	2.13-14 (//)	Thanks to God always*, 'brothers', chosen from the beginning
	B	2.15-17	'So then, brothers, stand...'; every work and good word
	B'	3.1-5	'For the rest, pray, brothers...'; love of God, patience...
A' (10 ¾ verses)	A	3.6-9	'Now we charge you, brothers...', the idle
	B	3.10-12	You were charged, work to eat, not walking idly
	B'	3.13-16c	'And you, brothers, do not lose heart doing good', obey

3.16d-18 (abb') Closing Greetings: 'The Lord be with...'; Paul's own greeting; 'The grace...be with...'

Notes:
It will be seen that the two 'halves' similarly begin, at 1.3 and 2.13, with nine Greek words common to them both (see below, for 1.3).* ***This is, of course, most significant!* *It is further evidence that rhetorical analysis when coupled with parsing clearly establishes a writer's endeavours. (In the Commentaries I have with me here in Jaffna, there is no recognition of this duality.)*
It was only during my second parsings of these two letters that I noticed the ***'brother' introductions*** *of so many pieces: 14/18 in the first; 7/12 in the second. How blind we can be!*

Below is the parsed Opening Greetings for this letter, for comparison with that of I Thessalonians. Immediately following both, as so often with Paul, the theme is thanksgiving.

1.1-2

Paul — a
        and Silvanus
        and Timothy,
    to the church of Thessalonians — b
        in God our Father
        and Lord Jesus Christ,
    grace to you — b'
            and peace
        from Father God
        and Lord Jesus Christ.

1.3...

Εὐχαριστεῖν ὀφείλομεν τῷ θεῷ πάντοτε περὶ ὑμῶν, ἀδελφοί, ..., ὅτι ...

To give thanks we ought, to God always concerning you, brothers,..., because...

I TIMOTHY

The structure of this letter is a seven section chiasm, here represented by 1,2,3,C,3',2',1', where each section comprises parts ABB':ABB'. Each of these further breaks down into three parts, abb', which, in the main, further break down into three parts each, .a.b.b'.

1.1-2 (abb') Introductory Greetings: from Paul; to Timothy; grace, mercy, peace

1.3-20	**Section I** (18 verses)			**Timothy's Task: to Warn False Teachers**
A (9 verses)	A	1.3-4	(abb')	Timothy in Ephesus: he is to charge those who teach differently
	B	1.5-7	(abb')	The end of the charge is love; not turned aside; law teachers
	B'	1.8-11	(//)	The law is good, used lawfully
A' (9 verses)	A	1.12-14		Paul thanks Christ who empowers him and has transformed him
	B	1.15-17		'Jesus came into the world to save sinners'; Paul: chief sinner
	B'	1.18-20		'This charge...', according to prophecies, a good warfare/conscience

2.1-15	**Section 2** (15 verses)			**Church Rules on Prayer**
A (7 verses)	A	2.1-2	(//)	An exhortation on prayers of all kinds
	B	2.3-4		'This is good...'; God wishes that all be saved
	B'	2.5-7		One mediator, a ransom; Paul teacher of Gentiles
A' (8 verses)	A	2.8-10		The way men should pray
	B	2.11-12		The way women should deport themselves..
	B'	2.13-15		...with good works

3.1-16	**Section 3** (16 verses)			**Rules on Church Appointments**
A (7 verses)	A	3.1-3	(//)	Oversight: Bishops, their qualities
	B	3.4-5		Ruling his household well
	B'	3.6-7		Not a new convert
A' (9 verses)	A	3.8-10		Deacons: similar qualities
	B	3.11-13		(Their) wives' qualities; Deacons ruling households,
	B'	3.14-16		'These things I write to you...'; concerning God's household

4.1-16	**Section C** (16 verses)			**Against False Teachings; Give a Good Lead**
A (10 verses)	A	4.1-5	(//)	The Spirit: in the latter days, some will depart from faith and truth
	B	4.6-9		'These things suggesting...', a good minister of Christ; on 'exercise'
	B'	4.10		Labour and struggle, hope on God, the Saviour of all
A' (6 verses)	A	4.11-12		'Charge these things and teach...', be a pattern, though young
	B	4.13-14		'Until I come attend to the reading..., do not neglect your gift
	B'	4.15-16		'These things attend to...', take heed to yourself and teaching

5.1-16	**Section 3'** (16 verses)			**Rules on Church Listings of Widows**
A (8 verses)	A	5.1-3	(//)	Older/younger men/women; widows - 'really widows'
	B	5.4-7		Widows: family support; the 'really widow', '...these things charge...'
	B'	5.8		Those not providing support for their own
A' (8 verses)	A	5.9-10		Let widows be listed, not less than sixty years...
	B	5.11-15		Younger widows
	B'	5.16		Believers with widows are to support them, not the church

5.17-6.5	**Section 2'** (14 verses)			**Church Rules on Elders, Sinners, Laying on of Hands**
A (6 verses)	A	5.17-18	(//)	Elders who rule well deserve double stipend
	B	5.19-20		If an elder is accused, reprove before everyone as a warning
	B'	5.21-22		Do not prejudge; do not be quick to lay hands on anyone, keep yourself pure
A' (8 verses)	A	5.23-25		Drink a little wine; some sins are clear beforehand, good works too
	B	6.1-2		Slaves, their masters and believing masters, 'These things teach and exhort...'
	B'	6.3-5		Those teaching differently are puffed up, supposing gain

6.6-21c	**Section 1'** (16 verses)			**Real Wealth; Against False Teachings**
A (7 verses)	A	6.6-7	(//)	Piety with self-sufficiency is great gain; nothing in/nothing out of this world
	B	6.8-10		Being simply satisfied; those resolving to be rich...; 'the root of evil...'
	B'	6.11-12		'But you, O man of God, flee these things', lay hold on eternal life
A' (9 verses)	A	6.13-16		'I charge before God, the one giving life...', be without reproach
	B	6.17-19		'To the rich in the present...', a charge not to be high minded...
	B'	6.20-21c		'O Timothy, guard the deposit...', from empty and false knowledge

6.21d Closing Grace

II TIMOTHY

The structure of this letter is a four section chiasm, ABB'A', where each section comprises parts ABB', which each further breaks down into three parts, abb'.

1.1-2 (abb')				Introductory Greetings: from Paul; to Timothy; grace, mercy, peace
1.3-18	**Section A** (16 verses)			**Encouragement to be Faithful**
	A	1.3-7	(abb')	'I thank God...', remembering and recalling Timothy
	B	1.8-12	(abb')	Do not be ashamed: to testify, or of Paul, prisoner
	B'	1.13-18	(//)	Keep to sound teaching; deserted; supported
2.1-19	**Section B** (19 verses)			**Encouragement to be an Approved Workman**
	A	2.1-7	(//)	Be strong, accept the cost, train, serve, receive...
	B	2.8-13		Remember Jesus Christ raised...; suffering, salvation
	B'	2.14-19		Remind, warn, be approved; avoid godless chatter
2.20-3.17	**Section B'** (24 verses)			**Encouragement to be a Noble Instrument**
	A	2.20-26	(//)	Keep clean; flee youthful desires, be gentle to opposers
	B	3.1-9		Be prepared for the terrible times of the last days
	B'	3.10-17		Keep to Paul's teaching, be strengthened in Scriptures
4.1-18	**Section A'** (18 verses)			**Encouragement to be Faithful in Ministry**
	A	4.1-5	(//)	In view of the coming judgement, preach, correct, rebuke
	B	4.6-8		Paul's work is almost done and reward is ahead
	B'	4.9-18		Come; deserted, harmed; but the Lord gives strength
4.19-22 (abb')				Closing: Greetings and News; Call and more Greetings; Benediction

Note: *Again in this letter, the 'listings' well confirm the writer's three-part/abb' method:*

From Section B' and Part B, 3.1-9: 3.1-5b

And this know, A
that in (the) last days
grievous times will come
for will be men
self-lovers, money-lovers, boasters,
arrogant, blasphemers, to parents disobedient,
ungrateful, unholy, without natural affection,
unforgiving, slanderers, without self-control,
untamed, haters of good, betrayers,
rash, conceited, pleasure-lovers,
rather than God lovers,
having a form of godliness,
but the power of it having denied.

From Section B' and Part B', 3.10-17: 3.10-11

But you have closely followed of me A
the teaching, the conduct, the purpose,
the faith, the patience, the love;
the endurance, the persecutions, the sufferings,
which happened to me
in Antioch, in Iconium, in Lystra,
what persecutions I bore,
and out of all,
the Lord delivered me.

TITUS

The structure of this letter is a three section formation, ABB', where each section comprises parts AA', which each breaks down further into three parts, abb'.

The Theme is: 'Doing what is Good'

1.1-4 (abb') Introductory Greetings: from Paul...; to Titus; grace and peace

1.5-16	**Part A**	(12 verses)		**Titus' Task Appointing Elders**
	A	1.5-9	(abb')	On Crete, appointing elders, the qualities expected
	A'	1.10-16	(//)	Able to counter rebellious people, circumcision party
2.1-14	**Part B**	(14 verses)		**What Titus is to Teach**
	A	2.1-8	(//)	Teach sound doctrine to old and young, men and women
	A'	2.9-14		Slaves: no to ungodliness/worldly passions; salvation
2.15-3.11	**Part B'**	(12 verses)		**What more Titus is to Teach**
	A	2.15-3.3	(//)	Teach these things; authorities; then also we...
	A'	3.4-11		But saved because of mercy; teach...; avoid quarrels

3.12-14 (abb') Closing Instructions: Sending, Calling, **Doing what is Good***
3.15 (abb') Closing Greetings and Grace

For 'doing.../loves.../teaches what is ***good***', see 1.8,16; 2.3,7,14; 3.1,8,14, for what appears to be a significant distribution.

PHILEMON

The structure of this letter is a three section formation, ABB', where each section comprises parts AA', which each breaks down further into three parts, abb'. It will be seen from the above chart that **Titus** and **Philemon** share the same structure.

1-3 (abb') Introductory Greetings: from Paul...; to Philemon and others; grace and peace

4-11	**Part A**	(8 verses)		**Paul's plea concerning Onesimus is based on love**
	A	4-7	(abb')	'I always thank my God... prayers'; your faith and love
	A'	8-11	(//)	Paul could demand, but he appeals on the basis of love
12-16	**Part B**	(5 verses)		**Paul is sending Onesimus back to Philemon**
	A	12-14	(//)	'I am sending him... back...'
	A'	15-16		Paul's reasoning, 'back'... 'as a dear brother'
17-22	**Part B'**	(6 verses)		**Paul's plea that Onesimus be welcomed**
	A	17-19	(//)	If a partner, welcome him; any charge is to Paul
	A'	20-22		Paul looks for 'benefit' from Philemon, is confident

23-25 (abb') Closing Statements: greetings; further greetings; grace

The purpose of this letter of Paul is to persuade Philemon to accept Onesimus back. The letter has style and much to commend it: it is beautifully written.

THE LETTER TO THE HEBREWS

The structure of this treatise is a five section chiasm, where each section comprises parts: ABB':ABB'. Each of these parts further evidences abb' parts which each break down still further into .a.b.b' parts.

The work is:

A Call: 1) To Recognize the Supremacy of the Son of God and his Eternal Covenant, and
2) To Persevere in Faith, Hope and Love:

Section I: 1.1-4.16 (64 verses) — **The Son, superior to Angels, to Moses; fix on Jesus, always the same, the Author of Salvation, witnessed to in the Old Covenant:**

A	1.1-14	(abb')	Final Revelation in the Son, superior to angels; always 'the same'
B	2.1-9	(abb')	Do not ignore your great salvation; all will be subject to him
B'	2.10-18	(//)	The Son and 'his sons', his brothers: for those who are tempted, he helps
A	3.1-15		'Fix your thoughts on Jesus'; Jesus is greater than Moses; no rest
B	3.16-4.5		God's rest – entering/not entering; hearing with faith
B'	4.6-16		A sabbath rest for the people of God; he was tempted: grace to help

Section 2: 5.1-7.28 (65 verses) — **Jesus, the superior High Priest, in the order of Melchizedek, Guarantor of a better Covenant; Continue in Love, Hope and Faith; Jesus made Perfect:**

A	5.1-10	(abb')	Priests identify with weakness; Jesus, made perfect; High Priest, of Melchizedek
B	5.11-6.3	(//)	Slow learners: elementary truths; move on to maturity
B'	6.4-12		No second beginning; God is not unjust; persevere in Love, Hope, Faith
A	6.13-20		Certainty of promise; God's oaths; hope – an anchor
B	7.1-16		Greatness of Melchizedek; imperfection of Levitical Priesthood
B'	7.17-28		A better hope; oaths: a better covenant; Jesus: eternal High Priest of one sacrifice

Section C: 8.1-10.18 (59 verses) — **Jesus, the superior Sacrifice, as Mediator of a superior New Covenant; the Old Covenant is obsolete and disappearing; a better Promise:**

A	8.1-6	(abb')	Jesus' Ministry and New Covenant are superior to the Old, a copy and shadow
B	8.7-13	(//)	The Old Covenant was unsatisfactory, the New made it obsolete, it is disappearing
B'	9.1-14		The first and second covenants compared; Christ's entry by his own blood
A	9.15-28		Covenants require a death; the old was a copy of a better sacrifice, once for all
B	10.1-10		The old order: a shadow; the new order: the reality; sacrifices and offerings compared
B'	10.11-18		Christ's sacrifice was once for all, for sin (remembered no more)

Section 2': 10.19-11.40 (61 verses) — **Continue in Faith, Hope and Love; better and lasting Possessions; a better Result; his people made Perfect:**

A	10.19-28	(abb')	A call to persevere: Faith, Hope, Love; encourage each other as the Day comes
B	10.29-39	(//)	Reminders of judgement; better and lasting possessions; not slipping back
B'	11.1-12		Faith: its definition and its early examples
A	11.13-22		They lived by faith but died before the promise; likewise later people of faith
B	11.23-31		Faith's further examples, with more 'Christian' interpretation
B'	11.32-40		Others, of faith, are commended for witness; all will be made perfect together

Section 1': 12.1-13.25 (54 verses) — **Persevere as others have done; fix on Jesus, always the same, the Author and Perfecter of the Faith and of the Eternal Covenant:**

A	12.1-13	(abb')	Surrounded by witnesses, 'fix your eyes on Jesus', the author of the Faith; discipline
B	12.14-24	(//)	Ways to live: you have come not to Mt. Sinai, but to Mt. Zion
B'	12.25-29		Take heed; for we are receiving a kingdom that cannot be shaken
A	13.1-8		Love: 'Entertain angels'; imitate leaders; Jesus is always 'the same'
B	13.9-16		Imitate Jesus in a life of sacrifice 'outside the city'
B'	13.17-25		Obey and pray for your leaders; an Eternal Covenant; receive benediction and greetings

Note: *This work is, without doubt, one of the finest compositions of the New Testament.*

A Sample of Hebrews, from Section 1', Part B: 12.14-24

(in a literal English translation of the Greek, to attempt a representation of a parsing of the Greek)

Follow peace with all men A
and the sanctification
without which no one will see the Lord.
Looking,
lest any (be) failing
of the grace of God';
lest any root of bitterness growing up disturb
and through this
the many be defiled;
lest any (be) sexually immoral
or a godless person
like Esau
who against one eating
gave up his rights of the firstborn.
For you know that indeed afterwards
wishing to inherit the blessing
he was rejected
for he found no place of repentance
though seeking it out with tears.

For you have not approached B
to a mountain that can be touched
and to one ignited with fire
and to darkness
and to deep gloom
and to whirlwind
and to a sound of trumpet
and to a voice of words
which the ones hearing
entreated
not to be added to them a word
for they bore not the thing being charged:
'If even an animal touches the mountain,
it must be stoned.'
And so fearful was the thing appearing
Moses said,
'Terrified I am,
and trembling.'

But you have approached B'
to Mount Zion
and to a city of (the) living God,
a heavenly Jerusalem,
and to myriads of angels,
to an assembly and church of firstborn
enrolled in (the) heavens
and to God judge of all men
and to spirits of just men made perfect,
and to a mediator of a new covenant,
to Jesus,
and to blood of sprinkling,
a better thing speaking than Abel.

JAMES

The structure of this letter is a four section chiasm. ABB'A' where each section comprises parts ABB', which in the longer form is ABB';ABB';ABB'. Each part of these further breaks down into three parts, abb', which, in the main, further break down into three parts each, .a.b.b'.

1.1	(abb')			Introductory Greetings: from James; 'to the twelve tribes'; greetings
1.2-27	**Section A** (26 verses)			**Faith; Trials; the Rich; Religion**
A (7 verses)	A	1.**2**-4	(abb')	'...my brothers', facing trials and testings, consider it pure joy
	B	1.5-6b	(abb')	Lacking wisdom? Ask God, believing
	B'	1.6c-8	(//)	The doubter shouldn't expect anything
B (10 verses)	A	1.9-11		The rich and humble; the rich will perish
	B	1.12-15		Persevering under trial, temptation not from God
	B'	1.**16**-18		'...my beloved brothers', good and perfect gifts come from God
B' (9 verses)	A	1.**19**-21		'...my beloved brothers', be quick to listen, slow to speak
	B	1.22-25		Listen to the word and do it
	B'	1.26-27		Religious? Real religion is action and keeping pure
2.1-26	**Section B** (26 verses)			**No Favouritism; Law; Faith and Deeds**
A (9 verses)	A	2.**1**-4	(//)	'My brothers...', show no favouritism between rich and poor
	B	2.**5**-7		'...brothers', poor insulted, rich exploiting
	B'	2.8-9		The Royal law: love your neighbour, no favouritism
B (8 verses)	A	2.10-11		Keeping the whole law
	B	2.12-13		You are to be judged by the law: being merciful
	B'	2.**14**-17		'...my brothers', faith, but no deeds, (no mercy)?
B' (9 verses)	A	2.18-20		Faith with and without deeds
	B	2.21-23		Evidence from the law: faith without deeds – useless
	B'	2.24-26		One who was righteous for what she did
3.1-4.10	**Section B'** (28 verses)			**Teachers: the Tongue; Wisdom; Worldliness**
A (9+ verses)	A	3.**1**-4	(//)	'...my brothers', teachers will be judged more strictly
	B	3.5-6		Illustrations and the tongue
	B'	3.7-10a		More illustrations and the tongue
B (8+verses)	A	3.**10b**-12		'...my brothers', these things ought not to be...
	B	3.13-14		One's wisdom is shown by deeds
	B'	3.15-18		Wisdom from above is peace loving
B' (10 verses)	A	4.1-3		So what of the fights and quarrels amongst you?
	B	4.4-6		Friendship with the world's ways is hateful to God
	B'	4.7-10		Submit to God, humble yourselves before him
4.11-5.20	**Section A'** (27 verses)			**The Rich; Patience in Suffering; Prayer and Sins**
A (13 verses)	A	4.**11**-12	(//)	'...brothers', speak not against, or judge your brother, God is judge
	B	4.13-17		Making money, boasting, sin of not doing what you know
	B'	5.1-6		A warning to rich people, (sin of) cheating others
B (5 verses)	A	5.**7**-8		'...brothers', be patient till the Lord's coming
	B	5.**9a**-c		'...brothers', don't grumble against each other
	B'	5.**10**-11		'...brothers', (don't grumble) remember the prophets
B' (9 verses)	A	5.**12a**-c		'...my brothers', swear not by heaven or anything at all
	B	5.13-18		Prayer and praying, sins forgiven
	B'	5.**19**-20		'My brothers', turning a sinner around... saves and covers sins

Notes:
*The biggest aid here to separating one unit from another is the writer's frequent use of the word **'brothers'** as an address at the head of a piece. It is used fourteen times in all, out of the thirty-six entries, at the Aa position. The abrupt no greeting, no benediction ending is noted, when compared with most of the other NT letters. For this feature as well as for structure, it compares with IJohn.*

I PETER

The letter is now viewed as having a four section ABB'A' form, where each section comprises parts ABB', or in the longer representative form, ABB';ABB';ABB'. Each of these parts further breaks down into three parts, abb', which, in the main, further break down into three parts each, .a.b.b'.

1.1-2 (abb') Introductory Greetings: from Peter; to God's elect; grace and peace

1.3-2.10	**Section A** (33 verses)			**Rejoice in your Trials: be Holy**
A (10 verses)	A	1.3-5	(abb')	Praise, mercy, hope..., an inheritance
	B	1.6-9	(abb')	Rejoice though you suffer trials, faith refined, salvation
	B'	1.10-12	(//)	Concerning this salvation, prophets spoke
B (13 verses)	A	1.13-16		"Therefore...', hope on grace, be holy
	B	1.17-21		Live lives as strangers; Christ the chosen, belief, faith and hope
	B'	1.22-25		Purified, love one another; the word has been preached to you
B' (10 verses)	A	2.1-3		Therefore, grow up, into your salvation
	B	2.4-6		Jesus: the living stone, rejected by men, chosen
	B'	2.7-10		This stone: to believers/unbelievers; a chosen people, holy nation
2.11-3.7	**Section B** (22 verses)			**Live Good Lives; Submit; Suffer only for Doing Good**
A (7 verses)	A	2.11-12	(//)	**'Beloved...'**, as strangers here, live good lives
	B	2.13-14		Submit to authorities, do right
	B'	2.15-17		God's will: do good; fear God, honour the King
B (8 verses)	A	2.18-20		Slaves submit to your masters
	B	2.21-23		To this you were called; as Christ suffered...
	B'	2.24-25		Jesus...; that we might die to sin, live for righteousness
B' (7 verses)	A	3.1-4		'Similarly wives, submit yourselves to your husbands'
	B	3.5-6		Consider the holy wives of the past
	B'	3.7a-c		Husbands, be considerate to your wives
3.8-4.11	**Section B'** (26 verses)			**Suffer only for Doing Good; The End; Submitted to Jesus**
A (9 verses)	A	3.8-9	(//)	**'Now the end...'**, be of one mind, called to inherit blessing
	B	3.10-12		Loving life and seeing good days, do good
	B'	3.13-16		Who is there to harm you if you are eager to do good?
B (6 verses)	A	3.17-18		Better to suffer for doing good; Christ died...
	B	3.19-20		Christ preached to the spirits..., saved through water
	B'	3.21-22		The saving water of baptism; all submitted to Christ
B' (11 verses)	A	4.1-3		Christ suffered in his body, you too
	B	4.4-6		Do not be judged by men, live to God; preached to the dead
	B'	4.7-11		The end comes; be clear minded, to Christ glory, Amen
4.12-5.14	**Section A'** (22 verses)			**Rejoice in your Trials: a Judgement**
A (7 verses)	A	4.12-13	(//)	**'Beloved...'**, rejoice in your trials, rejoice at the last
	B	4.14-16		Reproached for Christ, you are blessed, as a Christian
	B'	4.17-18		Judgement is begun with the household of God
B (8 verses)	A	4.19a-c		'So then...', commit to God and doing good
	B	5.1-4		'...therefore...', to Elders, an exhortation
	B'	5.5-7		to young men and all, an exhortation
B' (7 verses)	A	5.8-9		Beware of the devil, other brothers are suffering too
	B	5.10-11		'Now the God of all grace...', a benediction for sufferers
	B'	5.12-14		Closing: written, through Silas; greetings; peace

Notes:

Again, it has to be said, as for Hebrews and IJohn, that this is one of the finest compositions of the New Testament.

3.8, 'Now the end...': it is a subject starter (see 4.7 which begins the final piece of the Section, 3.8-4.11). It is not a 'finally'. It is not a letter conclusion. This phrase has confused not a few translators.

I PETER: a sample of parsing

It is taken from the beginning of the final Section which echoes the opening of the first Section:

Beloved, / do not be surprised / at the fiery trial among you,
for a trial happening to you,
as a surprising thing occurring to you;
but as you share
the sufferings of Christ,
rejoice,
in order that also
at the revelation of his glory
you may rejoice exulting.
If you are reproached in the name of Christ,
blessed (are you),
because the Spirit of glory and of God
on you rests.
For let no one of you suffer
as a murderer, or a thief, or an evil-doer,
or as a meddler in others' affairs;
but if as a Christian,
let him not be ashamed,
but let him glorify God
by this name:
because it is time
for judgement to begin
with the household of God.
And if......

An Earlier, now Superseded, Result of Analysing I Peter

1.1-2 (abb')	Introductory Greetings								
1.3-2.10	**Section A** (33 verses)								
A (10 verses)	A	1.3-5	(abb')	B	1.6-9	(abb')	B'	1.10-12	(//)
A' (9 verses)	A	1.13-16		B	1.17-19		B'	1.20-21	
A (7 verses)	A	1.22-23		B	1.24-25		B'	2.1-3	
A' (7 verses)	A	2.4-6		B	2.7-8b		B'	2.8c-10	
2.11-3.16	**Section B** (31 verses)								
A (7 verses)	A	2.11-12	(//)	B	2.13-14		B'	2.15-17	
A' (8 verses)	A	2.18-20		B	2.21-23		B'	2.24-25	
A (7 verses)	A	3.1-4		B	3.5-6		B'	3.7a-c	
A' (9 verses)	A	3.8-9		B	3.10-12		B'	3.13-16	
3.17-5.11	**Section B'** (36 verses)								
A (6 verses)	A	3.17-18	(//)	B	3.19-20		B'	3.21-22	
A' (11 verses)	A	4.1-3		B	4.4-6		B'	4.7-11	
A (8 verses)	A	4.12-14		B	4.15-16		B'	4.17-19	
A' (11 verses)	A	5.1-4		B	5.5-7		B'	5.8-11	
5.12-14(abb')	Closing Greetings								

As 'a result', this did look like a reasonably convincing summary of what might have been in the mind of Peter. The parsing of the concluding pieces was checked, however, and additional to this, further rhetorical considerations appeared necessary. Key opening words like 'Beloved' (2.11 and 4.12) were not both convincingly sited in the scheme. And the AA':AA' sectional structure worked in some places quite well, but in other places not so well at all. Some sub-sections looked as though they related to each other better as ABB' arrangements (consider for example: 2.11-17;18-25;3.1-7, for 'submission'). What appears immediately above is a record of but a step taken, a stage reached, mid-analysis, which employs both rhetorical analysis and parsing.

II PETER

The structure of this letter is a three section ABB' form, where each section comprises parts A:A', or in the longer representative form, ABB':ABB'. Each of these parts further breaks down into three parts, abb', which, in the main, further break down into three parts each, .a.b.b'.

The Letter focuses on **'Warning Believers about False Teachers'**

1.1-2 (abb') Introductory Greetings: from 'Simon Peter'; to those with faith; grace and peace

1.3-21	**Section A**		(19 verses)	**Everything for Life and Godliness**
A	A	1.3-4	(abb')	Knowledge, promises, escape from corruption
	B	1.5-9	(abb')	Add to faith: goodness, knowledge, love...
	B'	1.**10**-11	(//)	'Therefore,...brothers', make your calling and election sure
A'	A	1.12-15		Always reminding you, established in truth
	B	1.16-18		Not told cleverly invented stories
	B'	1.19-21		Scripture: men told what God wanted
2.1-22	**Section B**		(22 verses)	**False Teachers**
A	A	2.1-3	(//)	Beware false teachers and their influence
	B	2.4-8		Angels and others not spared judgement
	B'	2.9-11		The righteous are rescued; angels and false teachers
A'	A	2.12-16		'But these men...' will be paid back
	B	2.17-19		'These men...': what they are like
	B'	2.20-22		They are worse off than at the beginning
3.1-18	**Section B'**		(18 verses)	**The Day of the Lord**
A	A	3.1-4	(//)	'...beloved', wholesome thinking for the last days
	B	3.5-7		By God's word the world was made, sustained, will burn
	B'	3.8-10		The Day of the Lord will come; the Lord's patience
A'	A	3.11-13		Live accordingly, holy and Godly lives
	B	3.**14**-16		'...beloved', looking forward to the day, the Lord is patient
	B'	3.**17**-18		'...beloved', be on your guard, for lawless men, glory to Christ

Note: *The parsing of this letter well demonstrates this writer's superior competency, refinement and consistency in his writing method. (This Letter, like James', includes no closing greetings.)*

For a sample of parsing, we turn, as for I Peter, to the opening of the final Section:

This now, A
beloved,
is the second letter I write to you,
in which I rouse of you,
by reminder,
the sincere mind,
to remember
the words previously spoken
by the holy prophets
and your apostles' command
of the Lord and Saviour.
This firstly knowing,
that there will come
in the last days
in mocking,
mockers,
according to their own evil desires going,
and saying,
Where is the promise of his coming?...

I JOHN

The structure of this treatise is a four section chiasm, ABB'A', where each section comprises parts ABB', which in the longer form is ABB';ABB';ABB'. Each part of these further breaks down into three parts, abb', which, in the main, further break down into three parts each, .a.b.b'. (Compare James for form.)

1.1-2.14	**Section A** (24 verses)			**The Witness; God is light; Living in the Light**
A (10 verses)	A	1.1-4	(abb')	'What was from the beginning...', beheld, bear witness
	B	1.5-7	(abb')	'And this is the message...', God is light
	B'	1.8-10	(//)	"But if in the light we walk...', fellowship, sin's remedy
B (8 verses)	A	2.1-2		'My children...', he writes that we do not sin
	B	2.3-6		'And by this we know...', keeping the commandments
	B'	2.7-8		'Beloved...', commandments, old and new
B' (6 verses)	A	2.9-11		Living in the light, or darkness
	B	2.12-13		'I write...', children, fathers, young men
	B'	2.14		'I wrote...', children, fathers, young men

2.15-3.10	**Section B** (25 verses)			**Love not the world**
A (7 verses)	A	2.15-17	(//)	'Do not love the world...'
	B	2.18-20		'Children...', the time is short, antichrist is coming
	B'	2.21		'I wrote not to you because you do not know the truth...'
B (9 verses)	A	2.22-25		'Who is the liar...?' The antichrist
	B	2.26-27		'These things I wrote...', the anointing, not to stray
	B'	2.28-3.1		'And now, children...', of righteousness, children of God
B' (9 verses)	A	3.2-3		'Beloved, now children of God we are', pure
	B	3.4-6		'Everyone doing sin...', everyone sinning...
	B'	3.7-10		'Children...', do not stray, everyone not doing right...

3.11-4.13	**Section B'** (27 verses)			**Love one another**
A (7 verses)	A	3.11-12	(//)	'For this is the message...', love one another
	B	3.13-15		'Do not marvel, brothers, if the world hates you...'
	B'	3.16-17		'By this we have known love...', for the brothers...
B (10 verses)	A	3.18-20		'Children, let us not love in word, nor in the tongue...'
	B	3.21-24		'Beloved, if our heart...', confidence with God
	B'	4.1-3		'Beloved, do not believe every spirit...'
B' (10 verses)	A	4.4-6		'You are of God, children..., Spirit of truth and... error'
	B	4.7-10		'Beloved, let us love one another...', God's love is in us
	B'	4.11-13		'Beloved, if God so loved..., we also ought to love one another

4.14-5.20	**Section A'** (28 verses)			**The Witness; God is love; and Eternal Life**
A (8 verses)	A	4.14-16b	(//)	'... beheld and bear witness...',Son, Saviour of the world
	B	4.16c-18		'God is love...', love perfected, confidence in the day...
	B'	4.19-21		'We love because he first loved us...', the one loving God
B (12 verses)	A	5.1-4		Everyone believing that Jesus is the Christ..., the world
	B	5.5-8		'...overcoming the world? believing: the threefold witness
	B'	5.9-12		'If the witness of men we receive, God's witness is greater
B' (8 verses)	A	5.13-15		'These things I wrote...', that you may know... life eternal
	B	5.16-17		Asking for an erring brother: sin and mortal sin
	B'	5.18-20		'We know...': the one of God; the world; eternal life

Notes:

5.21 is not original to this work: 5.18-20 is complete without it; hence also the treatise.
As I finished preparing the presentation above, the first time around, I was actually completing my task of preparing all my first summaries of all the Books of the New Testament. (John's other letters and Jude were completed before this, because for the web page they were the smaller!) It was New Year's Day 2004 and it was a particularly significant moment for me to savour, though it bothered me then and it still does: 'How is it that we have not been seeing all these (obvious) arrangements before now?'
*In this first letter of John, what particularly stands out for me is the composite message of the two middle sections: **'Love not the world: love one another'**. I've not seen that before!*

A Sample Parsing of I John: the opening lines

What was from the beginning, A
what we have heard,
what we have seen with our eyes,
what we looked upon
and our hands touched
concerning the word of the life
(and the life was manifested
and we have seen
and we bear witness
and we announce to you the life eternal
which was with the Father
and was manifested to us),
what we have seen and heard
we announce also to you
that you also may have fellowship with us
and indeed our fellowship is with the Father
and with the son of him,
Jesus Christ,
and these things we write to you
that our joy may be complete.

And this is the message B
which we have heard from him
and we announce to you
that God is light
and in him is no darkness at all.
If we say we have fellowship with him
and in the darkness walk,
we lie
and *do* not the truth.
But if we in the light walk,
as he is in the light
we have fellowship with each other
and the blood of Jesus his son
cleanses us from all sin

If we say that we have no sin B'
ourselves we deceive
and the truth is not in us.
If we confess our sins
faithful he is
and righteous
that he may forgive our sins
and may cleanse us from all unrighteousness.
If we say that we have not sinned,
a liar we make him
and his word is not in us

My children, (*here, the next three-part presentation begins*) A
these things I write to you
in order that you do not sin
and if anyone sins,
an advocate we have with the Father,
(the) righteous Jesus Christ
and he is a propitiation concerning our sins…

II JOHN

The main structure of this letter is ABB', where each part comprises three parts, abb'.

The letter advises that commandments and teachings be followed, because deceivers are about.

vv.1-3 (abb') Introductory Address: from the Elder; 'to the chosen lady'...; grace, mercy, peace

vv.4-6	**Part A**		
	a	4	Rejoices at children walking in truth according to commandment
	b	5	Requests: the commandment from beginning, love one another
	b'	6	Love is walking in the commandments, this commandment
vv.7-8	**Part B**		
	a	7a	Because there are deceivers
	b	7b-c	They are saying Christ did not come in flesh
	b'	8	Beware, lest you lose your reward
vv.9-11	**Part B'**		
	a	9	Remaining, not remaining in the teaching
	b	10	Anyone without this teaching, do not receive or bid them farewell
	b'	11	To bid farewell is to share in their evil

vv.12-13 (abb') Closing Sentences: much to write; but hoping to be there; sister's children greet

III JOHN

The main structure of this letter is ABB'A', where each part comprises three parts, abb'.

The letter encourages Gaius to continue doing the good that he does, for which the Elder has witness, and to follow the good.

v.1 (abb') Introductory Address: from the Elder; to his friend Gaius; whom he loves in truth

vv.2-4	**Part A**		
	a	2	'Beloved...', prayers that he prospers
	b	3	He rejoices at the witness to his walking in truth
	b'	4	No greater joy than that his children walk in truth
vv.5-8	**Part B**		
	a	5	'Beloved...', is faithful in what he does for brothers/strangers
	b	6-7	they have witnessed about him and his sending them forward
	b'	8	We should entertain such men and be co-workers in the truth
vv.9-10	**Part B'**		
	a	9	'I wrote something to the church...', but Diotrephes...
	b	10a-c	'Therefore, if I come...', I will remember his works and words
	b'	10d-f	'And not being satisfied...', he does not receive brothers...
vv.11-12	**Part A'**		
	a	11	'Beloved, imitate not the bad, but the good...'
	b	12a-c	'To Demetrius, witness has been borne by all and truth
	b'	12d-f	'And we also bear witness and our witness is true

vv.13-14 (abb') Closing Sentences: much to write; but hoping to be there; peace and greetings

JUDE

The main structure of this letter is a scheme of seven parts, which appears to be describable as ABB';X;ABB', like I and II Corinthians (see Mark and Matthew also, for other uses), where each part comprises three parts, abb', and where each of these in the main comprises three parts: .a.b.b'.

The letter warns of ungodly men among the believers in the church.

vv.1-2 (abb') Introductory Address: from Jude; to the ones, loved…; mercy, peace and love

vv.3-4	**Part 1** 3a-c/3d-f/4	**A**	'<u>Beloved</u>…': he was to write about salvation, but he rather has to write to get them to contend for the faith, because of godless men slipped in among them
vv.5-7	**Part 2** 5/6/7	**B**	He reminds his readers/hearers of the Lord's delivering his people out of Egypt, but destroying the unbelieving, also about angels and Sodom & Gemorrah
vv.8-10	**Part 3** 8/9/10	**B'**	Similarly, these godless men pollute themselves, reject authority and slander celestial beings; even archangel Michael did not accuse the devil, but these abuse all
vv.11-13	**Part 4** 11/12a-c/12d-13	**X**	Woe to them, going the way of Cain, into Balaam's error destroyed in Korah's rebellion; they are blemishes, selfish shepherds, like clouds…, trees…, wild waves…
vv.14-16	**Part 5** 14a-c/14d-15/16	**A**	Prophesied Enoch, a judgement of everyone, to convict the ungodly of their acts, their harsh words; these men are grumblers, follow evil desires, flatter for advantage
vv.17-19	**Part 6** 17/18/19	**B**	'<u>But you beloved</u>…', remember what the apostles foretold, about the last times, scoffers and the ungodly; these are the men who divide you, without the Spirit
vv.20-23	**Part 7** 20/21/22-23	**B'**	'<u>But you, beloved</u>…', build yourselves up in the faith, pray in the Spirit, keep in God's love, waiting for his mercy, be merciful, show mercy with fear, hate evil

vv.24-25 (abb') Closing Benediction: 'Now to the one…; to the only God…; before all the age…'

The closing verses are presented below:

The letter is carefully crafted in all its parts of three-part pieces, but the ending is a particularly well honed Benediction (with an additional, emphatic line at the end of each part).

Now to the one being able
        to guard you without stumbling
        and to present (you) before his glory unblemished
                with exceeding joy
    to the only God our saviour
        through Jesus Christ our Lord
        (be) glory, majesty, dominion
                and authority
    before all the age
        and now
        and into all the ages,
                Amen

THE REVELATION TO JOHN

The book essentially declares the message that God is in control and that all evil will be destroyed eventually. The structure of the work is **a chiasm of 7 sections of '7s'**, whereby each section includes an introduction and seven parts. Given Christian, first century interpretation of the meanings of 'numbers' (and there is much meaning in numbers in this book), the structure of the book itself expresses the belief of the Church in 'a perfect completion and fulfilment of all God's purposes'. As the book says: all the church needs to do is to remain true and faithful to the 'Lord Jesus'.

Opening and other references to lampstands and allusions to Zech. 4.2-3,v.11 suggest strongly that the writer had the Jewish *menorah* in mind as he chose his structure (see the final note below):

Prologue: 1.1-8 (1-3/4-6/7-8) **Introduction; Address and Greeting; 'Jesus is coming'**

Section 1: 1.9-3.22 The Messages to the Seven Churches
(63 verses) Intro./ parts 1-7 1.9-20 / 2.1-7; 8-11; 12-17; 18-29; 3.1-6; 7-13; 14-22

Section 2: 4.1-8.1 The Seven Seals
(60 verses) Intro./ parts 1-7 4.1-5.14 / 6.1-2; 3-4; 5-6; 7-8; 9-11; 6.12-7.17; 8.1

Section 3: 8.2-11.18 The Seven Angels with Trumpets
(62 verses) Intro./ parts 1-7 8.2-6 / 8.7; 8-9; 10-11; 12-13; 9.1-12; 13-21; 10.1-11.18

Section C: 11.19-15.4 Seven Visions
(60 verses) Intro./ parts 1-7 11.19-12.18 / 13.1-10; 11-18; 14.1-5; 6-13; 14-20; 15.1; 2-4

Section 3': 15.5-16.21 The Seven Angels with Plagues (Bowls of Wrath)
(25 verses) Intro./ parts 1-7 15.5-16.1 / 16.2; 3; 4-7; 8-9; 10-11; 12-16; 17-21

Section 2': 17.1-19.10 Seven Words of Condemnation on Babylon
(52 verses) Intro./ parts 1-7 17.1-6 / 17.7-14; 15-18; 18.1-3; 4-20; 21-24; 19.1-5; 6-10

Section 1': 19.11-22.7 Seven Final Visions
(60 verses) Intro./ parts 1-7 19.11-16 / 19.17-18; 19-21; 20.1-3; 4-10; 11; 12-15; 21.1-22.7

Epilogue: 22.8-21 (8-11/12-15/16-21) **Concluding Testimony: 'Jesus is coming'**

Notes:
A Full Parsing proved less important here in the analysis of the Revelation than, say, in the analyses of Mark, Luke, Acts and John. As with Matthew, the book is primarily based on a numerical/numerological scheme.
The above presentation includes only a very few revisions to that which was published eighteen years ago in Sliced Bread... (1988). *The sectional structure of this book was a reasonably simple matter to establish because of all the 'sevens'. What was key to completing the exercise was the discovering of the repeating formula of 'And I saw', Καὶ εἶδον, that the writer used in what I now designate his Central and Final sections. I was then able to determine the parts of what is now Section 2'. Though these vary, similarity helped in the majority of cases: 'And he said to me...'; 'And he says to me...'. At first, I viewed the whole seven section scheme as a linear one. But when I saw the parallels, in sequence, between the seven parts of Section 3 and the seven parts of what was up until then Section 5 (now designated Section 3'), I began to test the whole structure for a chiasm.*
No relationship exists between the Gospel of John and the Revelation to John as we find in Luke-Acts, though both books feature use of 'sevens' in a big way, and not only in their numbers of sections which are arranged chiastically. (See my note on John, on page 26.)
The menorah began life, in written terms, in the Book of Exodus. To Orthodox rabbis, it represents 'the life and light of God in the world'. In John's Gospel (a seven-section chiasm), we are distinctly told in the Prologue that 'Jesus is the life and light of God in the world'. Here in the Revelation, it would appear that we are being told that 'the Church of the Lord Jesus is now the life and light of God in the world'. The interpretation that attaches to the menorah appears to have undergone such a development.

A Sample Parsing of the Revelation, 18.11-20, the second half of 18.4-20

(The listing here, of 29 items, in Part A, is the largest and most complex of any in the New Testament.)

And the merchants of the earth / weep and mourn / over her, A
because their cargo / no one buys / any more:
cargo of gold and of silver
and of valuable stone and of pearls;
and of fine linen and of purple
and of silk and of scarlet;
and every type of citron wood,
and every article in ivory,
and every article of very valuable wood
and of bronze and of iron and of marble;
and cinnamon and spice,
and incenses and ointment and frankincense,
and wine and oil,
and fine flour and wheat;
and beasts of burden and sheep,
and of horses and of carriages,
and of slaves and souls of men.
And the fruit of you / of the lust of the soul / went away from you. B
And all the sumptuous things / and the shining things / perished from you.
And no more / by any means / shall they find them.
The merchants of these things
the ones having become rich from her
from afar they will stand
because of the fear of the torment of her,
weeping and mourning,
saying,
'Woe, Woe, the great city,
clothed with fine linen and purple and scarlet
and glittering with gold and valuable stone and pearl.
Because in one hour
was made desolate
such great wealth.'
And every sea captain,
and every one sailing to a place
and sailors
and as many as work the sea,
from afar they stood.
And they cried out,
seeing the smoke of her burning,
saying,
'What is like unto the great city?'
And they cast dust on their heads.
And they cried out,
weeping and mourning,
saying,
'Woe, Woe, the great city,
by which were rich / all the ones having the ships / in the sea
from the worth of her.
Because in one hour
she was made desolate.'
Be glad / over her, / heaven! B'
And the saints! / And the apostles! / And the prophets!
Because God judged / the judgement of you / by her.
(*meaning: God judged her judgement of you.*)

Parsing and Rhetorical Analysis

To complete my presentation, I draw attention to a particular matter which may, or may not, have become apparent through the pages of this booklet. Parsing and rhetorical analysis work equally well together at both micro and macro levels. I will illustrate my point firstly with another look at the two books of the Gospel of John and the Revelation to John, and secondly with a look at the 'centres' of the New Testament Books.

Illustration 1: the Gospel of John and the Revelation to John

I present below two artworks that were first created in 1989. The one on the Revelation to John has been revised, the one on John's Gospel has not. I will go into my reasons shortly.

With the Revelation, my recent parsing attempts have required only minor revisions to the scheme that satisfied me (and all the literary-structural criteria I identified then) in 1988. They are found in those sections of the book, basically, that are outside of the numerical/numerological scheme, in the Prologue and the Epilogue. Parsing has disclosed that the Prologue is a three-part presentation: ABB', with verses: 1.1-3; 4-6; 7-8, where each part breaks down further into three parts, abb'. In this case, *the limits* of the Prologue are unchanged from before. Parsing disclosed also that the Epilogue is a three-part scheme: ABB', with verses: 22.8-11; 12-15; 16-21, where each part breaks down further into three parts, abb'. Before parsing, I viewed the Prologue and the Epilogue as consisting of two parts each, and the Epilogue as having limits 22.6-21. Verses 22.6,7 have now been added to the preceding Section 1'. Furthermore, this new ending to Section 1' now exhibits similar characteristics to the ending of the section that precedes it, Section 2'. In regard to these verses, 22.6,7, rhetorical analysis confirms the results of parsing. But in regard to the book as a whole, parsing affected no really significant change to my earlier rhetorical analysis.

My artwork on John's Gospel is unrevised. Because so many minor changes have been made to my earlier summary of the literary-structure of John's Gospel, the artwork is in need of redrawing, not totally, but significantly. What my old chart represents is the result of my rhetorical analysis of the book up to 1988. In the latter half of September 2003, I carried out my first parsing of this book. It had a major effect, though not at all on my understanding of the book's sectional scheme, nor upon my understanding of the form of the sectional structures (all ABB'/ABB':ABB'/ABB'). It was that many of the pieces that made up the sections were being differently identified. (I did decide too to go with early manuscript evidence and drop 7.53-8.11 from any reconstruction of mine of the original text, though there is a case for considering its inclusion.)

It was the discovery of the writer's style in the Prologue (1.1-18) which set me on my way parsing to establish the writer's *abb'* divisions of his text. Parsing also threw light on other aspects of the writer's rhetorical discipline, in particular the writer's predilection for repeating opening phrases to define the parts with which he made up his wholes. (I have said above that parsing John was a delight.)

It may be, if you compare my old artwork with my new chart (on page 26), that at first you will think that I have taken some backward steps. I am concerned enough myself to revisit the book for a second parsing. But I do recall the thought I had when reaching the final section, 18.28-21.25, and the closing half in particular, 20.1-21.25 (a whole in itself, but a balancing one for 18.28-19.42). The thought that came to me startled me. Yes, it was a shock to think that on Easter Day over all these years, in our churches, we may never have been reading the appointed Gospel in the way that the writer intended. John 20.1-18 is the appointed Gospel reading. In my old summary of literary-structural analysis, 20.1-18 is shown as the first of three parts: 20.1-18;19-29;30-31. Parsing persuaded me that the three parts are in fact 20.1-13;14-29;30-31. I am having to look at them again, even now, as I write this!

Essentially, 20.14-29 can be seen to be a three-part whole, where the two *appearances* of Jesus in the Upper Room are B and B' parts (satisfying the criteria for B being the first development and B' being the second and completing development) and where Jesus' *appearance* to Mary is the opening part A. The ending of the A part is suggested then as 20.18, because the B part clearly begins with 20.19. Rhetorical analysis was showing up also the writer's significant use of an opening phrase: at 20.14, ταῦτα εἰποῦσα (see, including variations: 6.59, 7.9, 8.20,30, 9.6,22, 10.6, 11.11,28,43, 12.36b,41, 13.21, 14.25, 15.11,17, 16.1,25, 17.1, 18.1 and 21.19b). Rhetorical analysis showed too the repeat of 20.2's content at 20.13 (an *inclusio*). This passage on the 'Empty Tomb' parses into an ABB' whole with three pieces per part. All three parts of 20.14-29 (20.14-18; 19-23 and 24-29) parse into three parts. What do I draw from all this, besides the fact that we have been reading to our *own* design? That '*seeing and believing*' is the B issue, and '*believing*' the B' issue, of 20.19-23 and 24-29 respectively. And that the writer of this Gospel intended a dramatic pause before v.14, a new beginning.

Illustration 2: the 'Centres' of the New Testament Books

In the earliest stages of my literary-analytical work, when I was simply looking for 'signifiers of structure' in texts, I was frequently finding something special at, or around, book centres.

Specifically, I found in Mark's Gospel, just after the central point, between the two middle sections, Sections B and B', the piece, 8.27-30 (of 8.27-9.1, a Day's telling). It is, of course, Mark's highly significant disclosure, in the mouth of Peter: 'You are the Christ'. It was only after a full rhetorical analysis and parsing that I saw a possible further significance. What appeared to be the title of the book, at 1.1, presented a problem. Was the phrase, 'Son of God', original to the opening verse, or not? (Early manuscripts declare only: 'Beginning of the Gospel of Jesus Christ'.) Given that this immediately post-central Gospel piece focuses only on 'the Christ', the likelihood is that 1.1 so focused only too. Mark could have given Peter two identities of Jesus to utter, but he chose not to, unlike Matthew, who wrote later, in Mt. 16.17: 'You are the Christ, the Son of the living God'. (Mark reserved his use of this status of Jesus to the next Day's telling (9.2-29): it is left to God himself to say, "This is my beloved Son…'.)

With the Gospel of Luke, an analysis for structural signifiers showed verses 13.31-35 to be the significant centre to the Gospel (Jerusalem: Jesus is to be killed there). Likewise, as I examined the Acts of the Apostles another significant centre was discerned, in 13.42-47 (here Paul and Barnabas say, '… behold, we turn to the Gentiles.') Here also, at the centre of the Acts, is explanation of the book's scheme, which starts in Jerusalem, turns in Antioch and ends in Rome. [As I write this I am being bombarded by maggots, dropping from holes in my work-room ceiling! It's a little distracting.] The theme, 'Rejection by Jews', is common to both book centres. Parsing confirms that they are of the same AA' structures. Rhetorical analysis confirms the common use of an uncommon word, ἐρχομένη (the principal papyrus, P^{75}, so reads).

It was not until after I had carried out a full rhetorical and parsing analysis of Matthew's and John's works that I discovered particularly interesting features too in both of their book centres. I refer on page 22, to what I found in Matthew's Gospel. It does appear that Matthew was bringing 'old and new things' out from his treasure store. He likely viewed himself, therefore, as a 'teacher of the law, *discipled* in the things of the kingdom of heaven' (Mt.13.52). In John's Gospel, it is something a little different. (I refer to this on page 26.) Just after its centre, in 11.1-10 and in its closing three-part, abb' piece, in Jesus' mouth are these words, 'Are there not *twelve* hours of the day? If anyone walks in the day… If anyone walks in the night…' Here, the rhetor is likely indicating why he chose to present his Gospel sections in *twelve parts*. Each part symbolizes an hour of 'daylight'. Elsewhere in the Gospel, Jesus is, clearly, the life and light of God in the world.

In the central section of the Revelation to John, key book themes converge in visions of victory over evil, judgement and salvation. The section concludes: God's 'righteous acts have been revealed'. At the conclusion of the central section of Paul's and Tertius' Letter to the Romans is a glorious ending which parses beautifully. And just after the central 'point' of IIThessalonians (a two-section presentation), the opening section's beginning is repeated in the second section's beginning (compare pieces: 1.3-5 and 2.13-14). The chiastic structure of Hebrews does not disappoint for the contents and emphases of its central section.

To the rhetors of the New Testament Books, the 'centres' of their works were a very important focus. A rhetorical analysis and a parsing of these 'centres' and the Books in their entirety expose the various, theological, soteriological, evangelistic and Christological interests, *as also* the literary intentions, of all the writers.

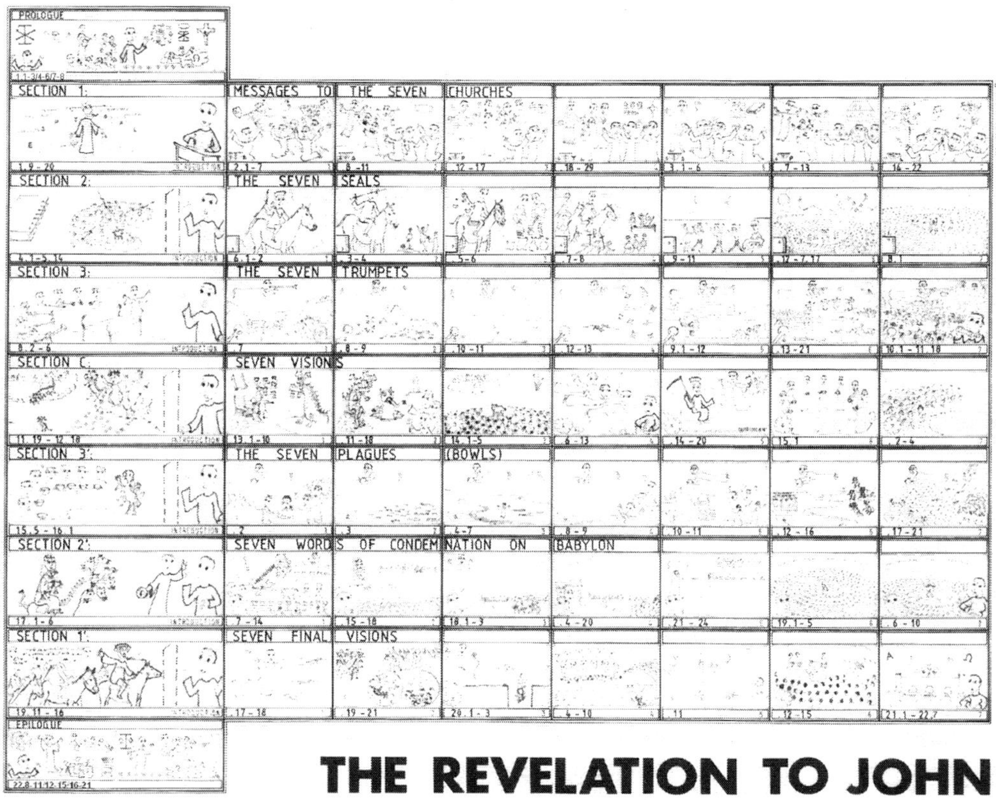

THE REVELATION TO JOHN

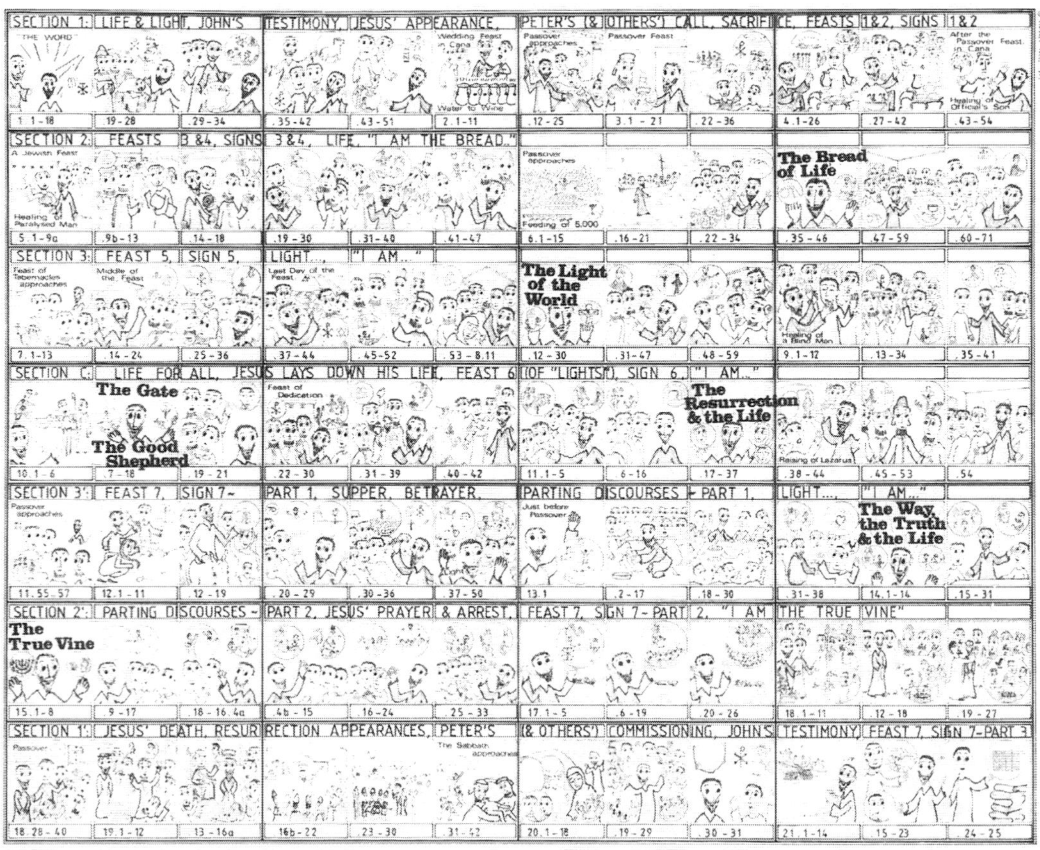

JOHN'S GOSPEL

What now?

Reading and studying the New Testament

This booklet facilitates a 'reading' of any New Testament book in the way that its writer and rhetor first intended. As 'readers', we now have the knowledge that the first reciters and readers had. The New Testament can be opened at any Book along with the appropriate summary page of this booklet and anyone can start reading for her/himself. Alternatively, Bibles can be marked up with information from this booklet. Or if you are one who has Bible software, you can select any book, copy it and then separate the text for yourself before reading it.

Clearly, it is best if you read the Greek. It is only in the Greek that you will see *all* the evidence. Bible editions present divisions in chapters and verses, editors' titles over separated texts, translators' separations of text and inconsistent translations of the same Greek words and phrases. All these *can* and *do* mislead the reader. If you can't read the Greek, learn Greek. If this is too much for you to consider doing, at the very least I suggest you get hold of an Interlinear Greek-English Version of the New Testament. It will help you.

No New Testament translation exists which reflects anything like the arrangements or the details of the Greek texts of the New Testament writers. It is scandalous? Yes! What is needed first of all, of course, is a definitive Greek text of the New Testament, laid out to the results of a full parsing and rhetorical analysis. The disk I have prepared to accompany this edition of this booklet is but a first step in this direction.

As we begin to master the art of reading the New Testament Books as their writers intended, so we will find that we have begun to study them in a new way. Sadly, however, little help is currently available. (Scholars will search this booklet in vain for the usual footnotes.) Yes, there are plenty of commentaries, but I do not know of one that is based on such a reading principle - reading a book or letter as the writer wrote it and intended it to be read. I am not saying, Don't turn to commentaries. There is much material, of course, of lasting value. But there is much that is contradictory and unhelpful and it will have to be put to one side.

New work abounds for New Testament scholars. There are discussions to re-open on the leading ideas of every Book and on the literary and theological abilities of every writer. There are both old and new questions to address. New commentaries are needed. And new translations in every language. An immense agenda is set.

Church scholars too will have their work cut out as New Testament studies impinge on all matters to do with doctrine and faith. These and all moral and ethical issues will (surely?) be approached with magnanimity now, given that it is hard to refute that all the writers of the New Testament Books were 'thinkers', each in their day and time, as we, constrained by limited science, fixed world views and cultural hang-ups, but journeying onwards all the same, in wisdom, in exercise of skills and in co-operation with the Spirit.

There is also another little matter: the Old Testament. Who is going to do a rhetorical analysis and full parsing of these Books?

My last point relates to the fact that the New Testament writers were conscious literary artists: it would be excellent to see their works reproduced in imaginative representations of every kind, especially ones in oils on large canvasses in famous galleries.

Keeping our heads

It may be that I will be making few new friends of New Testament scholars in the immediate future (see Appendix 2), but I'm not expecting that I'll be losing my head over all of this. The church has moved on from such times, yes?

Rather, what I'm thinking about is this as I close. Isn't it just possible (or am I so naïve) that *a new discipline* of New Testament study will be one in which we will be able to engage together, whether we are *currently* 'conservative', or 'liberal', or somewhere in between? The New Testament is very important to us all and it is of interest also to followers of other faiths and of none. But for Christians, the New Testament itself signals a unity in diversity, doesn't it? It is constant in its call for unity in Christ, even as it evidences process in its presentations of his person and the duties of his followers.

Or *am* I losing my head? May you keep yours.

Acknowledgements

All the New Testament writers are our teachers, but we each benefit from some of them more than others. It depends on who we are, what we're doing, and other factors. For me, Luke has a special place, because he started me on an intriguing journey. Mark too: he, more than anyone else, showed me *many* 'new things'. Paul and Tertius, likewise: because they showed me a new finishing line. But here, I want to express my gratitude to many other writers too who have had their influence on me. Especially, I want to remember and thank the scholars below. I list also their particular papers and books that stirred me in the earlier years of my investigations, by showing me 'new things' and awakening me to my task.

In order, from the beginning:

Bailey, K.E., *Poet and Peasant: A Literary Cultural Approach to the Parables*, Eerdmans, Grand Rapids, 1976

Talbert, Charles H., *Literary Patterns, Theological Themes and the Genre of Luke-Acts*, Society of Biblical Literature Monograph Series 20, Scholars Press, Missoula, Montana, 1974

Goulder, M.D., 'The Chiastic Structure of the Lucan Journey', *Texte und Untersuchungen* 87 (1963), pp.195-202

Fenton, J.C., 'The Gospel of St. Matthew', *The Pelican New Testament Commentaries*, Penguin Books, 1963

Tolbert, Mary Ann, *Sowing the Gospel: Mark's World in Literary-Historical Perspective*, Fortress Press, Minneapolis, 1989

Robbins, Vernon K., *Jesus the Teacher (A Socio-Rhetorical Interpretation of Mark)*, Fortress Press, Philadelphia, 1984

Mack, Burton L., *Rhetoric and the New Testament*, Fortress Press, Minneapolis, 1990

Drury, John, 'Mark 1.1-15: An Interpretation', in *Alternative Approaches to New Testament Study*, ed. A.E. Harvey, SPCK, London, 1985, also 'Mark', *The Literary Guide to the Bible*, Eds. Robert Alter and Frank Kermode, Collins, London, 1987, pp.402-417

For his exemplary method in displaying Greek text, in clauses:

Neirynck, Frans, *Duality in Mark: Contributions to the study of the Markan Redaction*, Rev. Ed. Leuven University Press, Leuven, 1988.

Throughout the years of my work, for his exemplary courage and integrity:

Strauss, David Friedrich, *Das Leben Jesu: kritisch bearbeitet*, 2 vols., 1st ed. Tubingen, 1835-36, 4th ed. Tubingen, 1840; tr. George Eliot, *The Life of Jesus Critically Examined*, SCM Press, London, 1973.

And for one very special moment of *many* in my work (see Appendix 2, p.iv):

Aristotle, *Ars Rhetorica* (*The Art of Rhetoric*, tr. J.H. Freese, Loeb Classical Library, Harvard University Press, Cambridge, Mass., 1926).

Appendix 1:

A Disquieting Time

For myself, the researcher and author of this booklet, it is a very disquieting time.

One moment I'm filled with the indescribable joy of having in my hands what is to me, even at this stage of my work, an unexpected treasure, unearthed from below the dusts of centuries of scholarship. I've had some of this treasure in my hands now for more than twenty years. But because of my investigations of recent months I can now see it all. All the treasure! It is awe-inspiring.

The next moment I am pinching myself to make sure I'm not dreaming. Also I worry that I might be making an utter fool of myself. That somehow I've got it all wrong. Lost my head! And then I try to think, even if this work is what I think it is, it's no big thing. I try!

I'm sad too. Sad for a variety of reasons. There's sadness mixed with anger, because what has been found should have been found a very long time ago. In fact it should never have been lost to the church in the first place! There's sadness mixed with perplexity. How could this have happened? Why the loss, for so long? And there's sadness mixed with bewilderment, because what has been found, if it had been found earlier, if it had never have been lost in the first place, would surely have had its influence for good in so many ways.

Questions haunt me. What might the church have looked like today? What might the church have sounded like in its doctrinal courts if it had always had this information? Wouldn't it have been more united in what it says about the New Testament? Wouldn't the church today, therefore, be more united than it is, in what it says and in what it does about its faith? I try to hold, however, to the joy that this newly unearthed treasure is everyone's now. I hold to the hope also of a new beginning for us all in the church (and on the fringes of it?) in the reading and the studying of the New Testament in the first place. I can be happy, very happy! But clearly, I can't be sure, and neither can you, or anyone, about where this will take us.

I'm aware that any challenge to our understanding is a challenge to our faith. And a challenge of this kind, as revealed in this booklet, doesn't pop up every day, thankfully! I know it will make its very heavy demands on us all. Yet, if we keep saying, and we should I think, that this treasure is of God, because it is and always has been an important but hitherto unknown element of the New Testament itself, we should not worry. In terms of both scholarship and Christian Faith it is always important that we journey where we are led.

Because of what is presented in this booklet, some may want to suggest that the texts of the New Testament have never before been examined so closely, or so carefully. It's for you and others to judge. For my part, I would deny that I've looked any more closely or more carefully than a host of others. Indeed, I'm much indebted to many for their expertise. But I count myself fortunate, or unfortunate, as the case may be, to have seen what they haven't seen.

With each piece of literary-analytical work that I did, I saw characteristics of the texts that had not been seen before. I knew, therefore, when I started tackling my next text, what I might look out for. It became a relatively simple exercise. But if I have brought anything new at all to the study of the New Testament it is a dogged persistence fuelled by an instinct that there were many things *still to be known* about the texts. This persistence ultimately rewarded me with the tools I needed to be able to do the analysis that I and others knew was needed.

It has been a stimulating and eventful journey for me over twenty-four years. There have been immensely exciting and rewarding periods in making discoveries, as in the last thirty months. There have been the inspirational times, and the longer 'perspirational' ones. There have been times also of great frustration, for lack of hours (due to my full-time ministry and other duties) and for reasons of my work being ignored by many scholars and publishers alike.

Until I have the careful and considered response of scholars to my work, I fear that I will continue to suffer the pendulum swings: to elation one moment and to despair the next.

Appendix 2:

I'm celebrating a few things...

This is a 'historical' piece. Written over a period of a few days and completed on the 31st October 2003 in Jaffna, this statement has since been edited only a little. A HEALTH WARNING is attached for any New Testament scholar reading it!

Since the British New Testament Conference at the beginning of September 2003 and my return to Jaffna, I have added to my previous two 'parsings' of Mark's and Luke's Gospels. Firstly, it was Matthew. Then it was Acts, then the turn of John. A start was made on the Revelation, a glance at IJohn, a little longer at IIIJohn and Jude, and then Romans. And what a delight it was, a complete surprise, being able to read 'Romans' in the way that Paul and Tertius had always intended it be read. Something that no one has done for centuries. And that is my point, my singular and all important point ('parsing' is simply a part of the method, an analytical tool). All these New Testament books can be read as their *authors* first intended. They are describable in ways that New Testament scholarship has simply not known anything about! There is no kind, or gentle way of putting it. *(On the 30th November 2003, I completed my first full parsing and rhetorical analysis of all twenty-seven books.)* Twenty-one years ago I started this work. In the few weeks since the British New Testament Conference it has come of age. There are structures. There is a style. There are things to be known beyond even the imaginings of most scholars.

My Methodology

Literary analysis, for me, begins with reading a text for its contents, emphases and themes and with looking, at the same time, for any signifiers of structure. This is the first stage of rhetorical analysis. Next to be explored are the writer's preferences for opening and closing formulae and any manner of method he might have used to signal the beginnings and endings of his passages. Sectional, sub-sectional and part propositions are raised in this way. These are then tested by a 'full parsing' of the text.

A full parsing of all the above books discloses that their writers employed the three-part presentational style, abb'. This means to me that we can accurately discern, as did the first readers/reciters, all the delineations of these writers' pieces which make up all the wholes and which together make up all the book wholes.

It is my judgement that these texts work at two levels, at what might be described as the 'public' and 'private' levels. At the 'public' level is that which is heard by the audience. We know it as the contents, that which was delivered from the mouth of the reader/reciter to the ears of the listeners. At the 'private' level is information the writer provided for the reader/reciter. Because it was then the writer's assistance to the one who would read/recite the work, it is today the assistance to anyone who might want to know *how* a book is written. And knowing *how* a book is written, of course, gives us sure knowledge of *what* is written. And knowing *what* is written, of course, gives us insight into understanding *why* it was written in the first place.

I do not exaggerate. This writing style allows us pinpoint accuracy. We can read whole texts in their parts, as they were first written. This is rudimentary information. It is basic to understanding these New Testament works. A study of church lectionaries demonstrates that many passages for Sunday reading both begin and end in places that the writers themselves would definitely not have chosen. New Testament scholarship in general is totally oblivious to the discipline of the writers. It is nothing short of shameful! It is scandalous!

It came to me, once back in Jaffna, after the British New Testament Conference of 2003, that I really did have a methodology that worked. I was able to do something that no one had literally been able to do for centuries. What had worked for Mark was then found to work for Matthew, and then for Luke-Acts as a whole, and wonderfully also for John. Book after book, I was completing work that over fifteen years ago had been published in *Sliced Bread*. But when it worked for me also on Paul, never having before looked into Paul's writings in this way, it was something, really something, the icing....! Reading Romans without sharp focus is one thing, but reading it in sharp focus, in full 3D and panoramic effect with surround sound, and for the first time, was something so special that it seemed to me it was worth living fifty-five years for just this one experience. But!

A Personal Critique of New Testament Scholarship

It is said: 'The New Testament *can hardly be considered as literature at all... The aesthetic motive and the desire to produce fine writing as something worthwhile in itself are foreign to its authors... The New Testament itself reveals little acquaintance with any literature other than the Old Testament... Their comparative indifference to pagan literature was on the whole an advantage to the writers of the New Testament. They gained therefore in freshness and freedom from stale conventions and artificial rhetoric...* ***They were not conscious literary artists, obeying a convention, and imitating the correct models, like Hellenistic authors,*** *but rather practical men falling into familiar forms when these happened to provide them with effective means of expression, in the case both of the oral and written literature.*' (From: 'The Literature and Canon of the New Testament', *Peake's Commentary*, reprinted 1977.)

One has to ask, How could anyone have got it so wrong? How could anyone (or everyone) have got it so *badly* wrong, and as badly wrong as this? Did the one who was writing these things not look at the New Testament texts himself to see if anything he was saying about them was actually right, or not? [Romans is a five section chiasm, 1,2,C,2',1', with sectional structures, ABB'/ABB'/ABB', as used in eleven other books.] And was there no one around to tell him that he had got it all wrong? [Matthew and Luke-Acts demonstrate 1-5,C,5'-1' sectional arrangements; John and Revelation: 1-3,C,3'-1' schemes.]

I am not normally led to consider possible conspiracy theories, or possible sinister motives, but with this I am! It is so incredibly badly wrong. [Mark's sectional structure shares the same arrangement as the book structure of Homer's *Iliad*, ABB',X,ABB', see *The Markan Matrix*, p.348.] Or, is it possible that Classics Scholars deliberately hid the truth, for good motives? Yes, of course, *good* motives! The New Testament had to be preserved from being associated with any *pagan* influences! I'm trying to believe in a conspiracy, trying very hard, but the less attractive alternative is I think the one that I am going to have to live with. The only possible position that I think can be entertained is simply that New Testament scholarship has been found wanting! It has never done its own homework!

I have had my own testing times with New Testament scholars! In 1988 when I put my work out in *Sliced Bread: the Four Gospels, Acts and Revelation; their Literary Structures* it was met with an academic's review, 'The Revelation to John maybe, *but not surely the Gospels*?' That's all! After all that work on sifting the structures and presenting the structures of the books! Yes, there was some appreciation of my 'scholarship', and an acknowledgement of all the work I had covered, but in the end the judgement hung on the reviewer's assumption: we have never seen anything like this before, so it cannot possibly be right! And when my next book *The Markan Matrix: a Literary-Structural Analysis of the Gospel of Mark* came out, in 1999, it did get a particularly long review in a thoroughly academic publication (*JTS*, vol.52, Apr. 2001). But all the reviewer could say, towards its close, was, 'Much as one respects the scholarship and conviction which has gone into this book, *sadly it runs counter to too many currents and consensuses* in Markan scholarship....' How does one answer this? What is this academic word, 'sadly'? For whom is one to be 'sad'? For me? Or are we to be sad for Markan Scholarship? And what of 'currents' and 'consensuses'? To whom are they important? The ones who are responsible for them!

I have a few more examples of the problems scholars have. A revered Professor I bumped into at the recent Conference, asked me (in regard to 'Mark'), 'You're the one, aren't you, who's interested in numbers?' I actually have no predilection for numbers, but I do note that Mark does (see for example Mk. 8.19-21). The Professor, *like many of us*, has a problem with 'numbers'. Another who became a good friend in Sri Lanka, now returned to Scotland, is a Professor of Applied Theology. After years in the work, like the aforementioned Professor, he cannot *believe* that there is anything more to the study of the New Testament than what *he knows* already. And in the last four weeks, as I've emailed my most recent findings to the relevant BNTC delegates (appropriate to their seminar groups and research interests), I have had the kind of response I might have expected: a deafening silence from the majority, and two replies from delegates requesting me to remove their names from my lists! I have had, however, the happy experience of a handful of what do seem to be sincere 'thank yous' and the not unexpected gentle and warm support of one (Methodist) Professor. The reason for the majority's silence? Busyness, most likely. But

New Testament scholarship has been so long without any factual, objective information about the texts that even now, when it is given such information, one wonders if it will be able to recognize it for what it is! New Testament Scholarship has been 'off the rails' for years.

I'm in my 56th year of life. I'm so thrilled to be excited about anything, I suppose. And here is something to make alive every fibre of my being! I'm angry too! Someone should have been able to tell me when I was a boy that Mark's Gospel was four series of seven days! The New Testament world of scholarship is naked, has no clothes! It has never *known* the New Testament books! I'm in my 25th year of ministry, my 21st year of serious New Testament analysis.

Just when we needed it most in the modern era, there was no one around to teach us rhetoric. We are having to learn about it from scratch, from our libraries. For me there was one particular moment of realization. I was standing in the Classics section of the Glasgow University Library. Aristotle's *Ars Rhetorica* in hand. The rules of the Epilogue: when you get to your *epilogos*, don't use 'ands' to begin your sentences. Don't use 'ands'... Don't use 'ands'! One of the *certainties* of modern scholarship is that Mark did not write Mark 16.9-20, and one of the reasons is that *it lacks* the *καὶ* (the 'and') with which he normally began his sentences! Inept, absurd, silly, unskilful! Ignorant! Has modern New Testament scholarship any foundational disciplines of any worth?

Just when we could have done with someone who really knew about parsing, there was again no one at all to help! Lost! The art and the science, the discipline... gone! My friend and Methodist Professor, however, persuaded me to think about my own definition. What was it that I was doing and was now calling 'parsing'? I turned to the Seventh edition of the Concise Oxford Dictionary (the only edition I have in Jaffna). And I found woefully inadequate definition there. For me parsing is to do with 'part'-ing, by which I mean that the function of parsing is first and foremost the discerning of the parts, by understanding them fully, as well as by understanding how they function in relation to other parts. It is an exercise not for its own sake, but for the sake of understanding a whole piece of literature in terms of all its parts. Certainly, it was not conjured up in the first place by Classics' Teachers with the intention of boring school students stupid.

And now perhaps we come to the strangest realization of all. We read that New Testament criticism *despairs* of all sorts of things that it says it *cannot know* about the New Testament books themselves. Yet, I simply do not believe this any more! For 'despairs of' read 'delights in'. Ignorance has been bliss! Just about any theory, or any fanciful idea ('Q' for one!) could be entertained, anything at all which could be conjured up for a legitimate exercise. But for all the frenetic activity, and for all the recent diversification of New Testament interests, where are the sure results? Consensuses are not quite the same, are they? And where in the list of research priorities is our exploration of the actual texts of the New Testament? At the top, where we might have expected it to be? Not according to what I have seen of the lists of post graduate research interests. How can we talk of New Testament scholarship as a 'discipline' in its own right, if we are not exploring the Greek of the New Testament texts and manuscripts? Is it the aforementioned 'despair' that led to the work's relegation?

And there is yet more. We speak of what we *believe* to have been the skills of past New Testament scholars, before the new critical era. But what I want to know is this: if they had had skills in rhetoric as we are led to believe, and if they had had skills in 'proper parsing', why...? Be patient with me. Let me try a little harder to shape the question in the clearest possible way. If the old disciplines of Rhetoric, of reading Greek and of doing proper parsing were all the stock-in-trade of past New Testament scholars, why (Yes! and Yes?), why were we not the recipients of handed down truths from them about the structures of the New Testament books and the styles of the New Testament writers that would surely have been known to them if we can know them now, using the tools that we thought were once theirs?! A discipline of study, even a disciplined study, cannot have failed in its task for so long, can it? The conspiracy theory has a lot going for it! The alternative is otherwise true: no one, for centuries has actually been reading the New Testament texts for themselves! No one has bothered him/herself enough to go back to the manuscripts and read them! They have let the years of scholarship cloud their eyes from seeing the scholarship of the New Testament writers for themselves. If you are one who has been reading the capital letters and the full stops in the texts you have been studying as the actual delineations of sentences that the writers 'clericals'. It got to 12.00noon. 'I'm going like this. I'm representing you and people like you', I said. And they'd just taught me to plaster.

The first term in Cambridge was one I would like to forget, but it all changed for me in the weeks after the Christmas break. I had to decide on the courses in which I would be examined. Because I thought myself too old at 33 to be preparing for exams, I opted for an Undergraduate thesis to relieve myself of one course. Immediately, I began glimpsing a work that needed attention. My focus was the structure and content of the Central Section of Luke's Gospel. (Lk. 9.43b-19.48 eventually defined the extent of it, for me.) I became acquainted with copies of the earliest manuscripts at the University Library. The Finals came quickly enough, too quickly! Besides the course work, there were services to prepare, daily prayers and duties as President of the Student Common Room, for the second time in my life. And there was my wife too, and our three young children then, a soccer team to play for and squash! (On the last day of the final term, the Methodist Secretary of Candidates for the Ministry joined us at Wesley House for evening dinner. I was able to thank him, very genuinely, for insisting that I studied for a theological degree in Cambridge.)

My family was in Hull the day of my last exam, having gone ahead of me. To celebrate my completion of the courses and the exams, after evening hall at Wesley House I went to my study room on 'A' staircase and ceremonially swept my last exam's books and papers onto the floor, from off the top of my desk with the back of my right hand. On the desk, I then placed my own special folder. Working till 4.30am on Mark's Gospel, I went to bed on a high. I knew before I left Cambridge that Mark's Gospel was likely Four Series of Seven Days, that Luke and Acts likely paralleled each other and that they and Matthew were likely eleven-section chiasms. I thought *then* that John was likely also an eleven-section chiasm. It was the summer of 1983, the summer of my Ordination, twenty years ago.

Λοιπὸν· ('For the rest...')

What had struck me in Cambridge was that there was a huge job still to be done on the Books of the New Testament. It was in fact very unsettling *knowing* that there was a lot more still to be discovered, that there were so many indicators of this. What struck me when I attended the British New Testament Conference in Birmingham (in 2003) was that there was still a lot left for me to do. And yes, I had wanted a chance to present a paper on my subject, but I hadn't been given it. I twice tried. I attended anyway from Sri Lanka and I'm glad I did. When I got back to Jaffna, apart from the work I do, nothing could have stopped me from getting back down to my own New Testament research.

Eight weeks have now passed and it has been another immensely exciting period in my life for making New Testament discoveries. I'm here on my own just now, a repeat of twenty years ago. Again, my wife is with the children, but this time Sue's in Scotland, for the birth yesterday, to Kenny and Rosalind, of our first grand child, Finlay James Hutchison. I raise this work to you Finlay! Your *amapa** salutes you! At least there's one little boy who's going to grow up knowing that Mark's Gospel is Four Series of Seven Days.

* *amapa* is Tamil for 'mother's father'

A Postscript (April 2006)

In 2003 and 2004, I attended the annual British New Testament Conference, from Sri Lanka. I gained a lot, each visit, though what I really wanted was an opportunity to share something of what was exciting me. (My pre-conference, e-mailed proposals of papers were not taken up.)

I was delighted, therefore, on my third attempt, to be given my first opportunity in 2005 to present, at the Liverpool Conference, on the methodology and results of my own New Testament research. The paper was well received by my seminar group. (I also gave out copies of my earlier edition of this booklet to others there.) But since then, I've heard nothing from anyone.

In the last year, I've had the 'usual' rejections from publishers, just as prior to 1988 and to 1999, and one after four months of hopeful waiting. The upside is that in this time the work has gone on improving. The downside is that I am having to self-publish again.

intended, you have not been doing your job. You never went back to the texts that the writers left us, in their 'sentence-less' *and* even wordless states!

Mark is a brilliant writer! He's no writer at all! I am on another tack now, into head wind! He's a wonderful theologian! He's no theologian! Opposite views are heard on just about everything in New Testament circles! (In regard to Mark, many views pertain simply because his work isn't understood for what it is.) No wonder New Testament scholarship is ridiculed in the pulpits of fundamentalist churches all around the globe. And we hear from their preachers, 'scholars say…', and 'theologians would have us believe…'.

In Sri Lanka at the present time 'an 'anti-conversion' bill is being presented in Parliament' and there is 'a sudden and unprecedented increase in violence against Churches, particularly the newer and smaller Churches, and pastors and workers' (in the south mainly, from a growing number of Buddhists; but also in the northeast, from a few Hindus). My quotes are taken from the Pastoral Letter, the National Christian Council, 17th October 2003. It is a complicated issue, but my judgement is that one significant component is rampant, un-checked, mainly western-style Christian Fundamentalism.

It may be that you will not like where this bit of my presentation is going. As clearly as I can I will say what I think ought to be said. Christian Fundamentalism is one outcome of failed New Testament scholarship. That the church itself is biblically naïve and theologically naked is also the result of failed New Testament scholarship. That the church itself is failing disastrously in the materialist culture it helped cultivate is due in no little way to the paucity of relevant help it has received from its New Testament scholars.

Some Personal Recollections

Am I to be accused of ranting? Maybe. But I'll tell you this, and you will no doubt believe me. I left my first three-year ministerial appointment very reluctantly to go to Cambridge University in 1981, to Wesley House and Fitzwilliam College. I kept putting off going and I was told in the end, 'If you don't go this year, you won't be going at all.' It was the then Methodist Secretary of Candidates for the Ministry who told me this. I'd been at All Nations Christian College in Ware for two years, on a shoe-string budget, and with a wife and two young children, and I'd then answered a call to serve as a 'lay minister' in Methodist Churches in Lower Holloway and Camden Town - rough, difficult areas, between 1978 and 81.

Leave the asylum seekers from El Salvador? The prostitutes? The drug addicts? The squatters? The Scotsmen who wanted to get back to Aberdeen? Leave an Irish Catholic Priest who could celebrate his 25th year of ordination, after the celebratory Ecumenical Service, in the School playground standing on a dais with a pint of beer in one hand and a fag in the other, and address us on his joys in priestly service? Leave churches that were growing? Leave three Methodist Churches that were growing in membership, attendance and relevance? Leave when we were working as churches and architect minister to renew and beautify the buildings, inside and outside? Leave when we were building accommodation for a Christian Community and Mission Team in residence in Camden Town? Leave and go to Cambridge and study academic theology?

I went. And for the first term it was basic Greek for me, also Source, Form and Redaction Criticism! Relevant? What! There was a degree to be had! I'd got a degree in Architecture. I was told I had to get one in theology too! Yes and after I'd taken seven years to register and practice as an Architect, another seven years of training had to be completed. But I'd done five, there were only two more to go, and I'd already completed the only necessary probationary year as a Pre-Collegiate probationer. I'd be ordained at the Middlesborough Conference, in Durham, after Cambridge. I committed myself to the task. Jacob, all over again!

My first four weeks in Cambridge were spent in Camden Town. The Beacon Hill manse off the Camden Road had to be vacated before the 1st September, but the building work hadn't been completed in Camden Town, so the church was my home during the week and Wesley House, Jesus Lane, at the weekends. I was working with a father and son building partnership. We used to rib each other a lot. That is, I learned to give as good as I got. One of my best moments with them was when I was due to lead worship at a Wednesday lunchtime service at Wesley's Chapel, our Methodist 'cathedral'. They were both anxious that at 11.30am I hadn't begun to change out of my working clothes into my